Trump and the Politics of Neo-Nationalism

No analysis of the Donald Trump phenomenon and American neo-nationalism is satisfactory without examining the impact of both the Christian Right and the secular nationalist right, both in the USA and abroad. This book analyses the political impact of both strands in relation to America's culture wars at home and the clash of civilisations in the USA's foreign policy.

Each strand – religious and secular – has had different issues to pursue during the Trump presidency: religious liberty and associated issues, on the one hand, and 'America's place in the world', on the other. This book demonstrates how both strands overlap and draw on each other's concerns to exhibit a pronounced, multifaceted neo-nationalism which was ideologically important for the Trump presidency. The author emphasises that the Trump phenomenon has been building for decades, and the Trump presidency has used significant political, social, economic, and cultural disquiet, and the post-2008 economic crisis and associated global turmoil, to fashion and progress policies which appeal strongly to both the Christian Right and many secular nationalists.

This book will be of interest to students, researchers, and policy-makers interested in American politics, American political history, religion and politics in America, and religion and IR with a focus on the USA.

Jeffrey Haynes is Emeritus Professor of Politics at London Metropolitan University, UK. His areas of expertise are religion and international relations, religion and politics, democracy and democratisation, development studies, and comparative politics and globalisation. His publications include more than 50 books, most recently: *Peace, Politics, and Religion* (ed. 2020), *Religion, Conflict and Post-Secular Politics* (2020), *The Routledge Handbook to Religion and Political Parties* (ed. 2020), and *From Huntington to Trump: Thirty Years of the Clash of Civilizations* (2019).

Innovations in International Affairs
Series Editor: Raffaele Marchetti
LUISS Guido Carli, Italy

Innovations in International Affairs aims to provide cutting-edge analyses of controversial trends in international affairs with the intent to innovate our understanding of global politics. Hosting mainstream as well as alternative stances, the series promotes both the re-assessment of traditional topics and the exploration of new aspects.

The series invites both engaged scholars and reflective practitioners, and is committed to bringing non-western voices into current debates.

Innovations in International Affairs is keen to consider new book proposals in the following key areas:

- **Innovative topics**: related to aspects that have remained marginal in scholarly and public debates
- **International crises**: related to the most urgent contemporary phenomena and how to interpret and tackle them
- **World perspectives**: related mostly to non-western points of view

Titles in this series include:

Trump and the Politics of Neo-Nationalism
The Christian Right and Secular Nationalism in America
Jeffrey Haynes

Russian Public Diplomacy
From USSR to the Russian Federation
Marina M. Lebedeva

International Perspectives on Public Administration
Henry T. Sardaryan

For more information about this series, please visit: www.routledge.com/Innovations-in-International-Affairs/book-series/IIA

Trump and the Politics of Neo-Nationalism

The Christian Right and Secular Nationalism in America

Jeffrey Haynes

LONDON AND NEW YORK

First published 2021
by Routledge
2 Park Square, Milton Park, Abingdon, Oxon OX14 4RN

and by Routledge
605 Third Avenue, New York, NY 10158

Routledge is an imprint of the Taylor & Francis Group, an informa business

© 2021 Jeffrey Haynes

The right of Jeffrey Haynes to be identified as author of this work has been asserted by him in accordance with sections 77 and 78 of the Copyright, Designs and Patents Act 1988.

All rights reserved. No part of this book may be reprinted or reproduced or utilised in any form or by any electronic, mechanical, or other means, now known or hereafter invented, including photocopying and recording, or in any information storage or retrieval system, without permission in writing from the publishers.

Trademark notice: Product or corporate names may be trademarks or registered trademarks, and are used only for identification and explanation without intent to infringe.

British Library Cataloguing-in-Publication Data
A catalogue record for this book is available from the British Library

Library of Congress Cataloging-in-Publication Data
Names: Haynes, Jeffrey, 1953– author.
Title: Trump and the politics of neo-nationalism : the Christian right and secular nationalism in America / Jeffrey Haynes.
Description: Abingdon, Oxon ; New York, NY : Routledge, 2021. | Series: Innovations in international affairs | Includes bibliographical references and index.
Identifiers: LCCN 2020053813 (print) | LCCN 2020053814 (ebook) | ISBN 9780367641665 (hardback) | ISBN 9781003122432 (ebook)
Subjects: LCSH: Christianity and politics—United States. | Nationalism—United States. | Nationalism—United States—Religious aspects—Christianity. | Religious right—United States. | Trump, Donald, 1946– Influence. | United States—Politics and government—2017– | United States—Foreign relations—2017–
Classification: LCC BR516 .H38 2021 (print) | LCC BR516 (ebook) | DDC 320.540973—dc23
LC record available at https://lccn.loc.gov/2020053813
LC ebook record available at https://lccn.loc.gov/2020053814

ISBN: 978-0-367-64166-5 (hbk)
ISBN: 978-0-367-64175-7 (pbk)
ISBN: 978-1-003-12243-2 (ebk)

Typeset in Times New Roman
by Apex CoVantage, LLC

Contents

	Introduction: Trump and the politics of neo-nationalism	1
1	From nationalism to neo-nationalism	19
2	Culture wars and neo-nationalism	36
3	Neo-nationalism and politics in the USA	52
4	Neo-nationalism and America's international relations	70
5	Conclusion: Donald Trump and neo-nationalism in America, 2016–2020	87

References 99
Index 113

Introduction
Trump and the politics of neo-nationalism

Donald Trump took the Republican Party by storm. Despite the odds being heavily stacked against him, he became the party's 2016 presidential candidate. Trump convinced tens of millions of Americans to vote for him despite having no political experience. What was Trump's appeal? For many Americans, especially male white conservatives, Trump had qualities that his opponent, Hillary Clinton, a close ally of President Barack Obama, lacked. He was 'pro-religion', put 'America First', and did not object to upsetting foreigners and rejecting international agreements if they were judged not to be in the USA's national interest.

Like Clinton, Trump divides opinion in the USA. Yet neither of them caused the political polarisation which characterises America. Out of power, Clinton is now politically inconsequential. Trump is both a proximate cause and a consequence of America's stark political disagreements. He is a proximate cause because of his manner, style, and social media engagement. He is a consequence of a long process of division, developing since at least the presidency of Ronald Reagan four decades ago. After a lull during the George W. Bush administration, Barack Obama's presidency brought fundamental political and social divisions to the fore again. For conservatives, Obama was too liberal, overly concerned with gender, sexual, and racial equality, and uninterested in the problems of white conservatives, especially Christians. Many believed that Obama was a Muslim and a foreign alien.[1] In short, Obama was the catalyst and Trump was the beneficiary of the USA's resurgent culture wars. Not necessarily initially pro-Trump, many conservatives voted for him in 2016 not only because they were 'anti-Hillary' ('Lock her up') but also because they liked Trump's nationalist policies: he was regarded as 'anti-establishment', anti-immigration, and 'pro-family'.

Trump sought to appeal to millions of American voters with a simple slogan: "Make America Great Again" (MAGA). But what did it mean? When was America *not* great? How do we measure 'greatness' in this context? 'Greatness' for whom? 'Greatness' for what? As a slogan, MAGA found favour with Trump's support base: white Christian conservatives and white less-Christian (and secular) 'America First' nationalists. What they shared was a yearning for the supposedly halcyon days of a prosperous white America, a 'return' to when the 'American dream' seemed for many realisable. For lots of white Americans this would be the post-war boom years: the 1950s and early 1960s. This was a time when white Americans were demographically in the majority, the USA enjoyed strong and consistent economic growth, and many (white) Americans experienced rising prosperity in a country seemingly galvanised by a get-up-and-go dynamism.

For many Trump voters, MAGA also implied a promise to deal with the allegedly corrupt administrative/bureaucratic system: referred to by Trump as the 'deep state' and 'the swamp' (Smith, 2020). For many white conservatives, MAGA underlined Trump's promise to return the USA to a position where the supremacy of their social and political worldviews would be assured: women know their place both in the workplace and at home; ethnic and racial minorities know their place in the social, political, and economic order and should not try 'too hard' to improve their existential positions via 'affirmative action'; and the USA is safe from external and internal attack, including the baleful influence of 'foreign' ideas: socialism, globalism, and Islamism. In addition, MAGA pointed the finger at another of Trump's *bête noires*: 'cheating' trading partners', including China, the European Union, Canada, Mexico, and Turkey. His claimed justification was that America's trading partners swindled America via unequal trading relationships, and as a result the USA haemorrhaged well-paid, skilled, and semi-skilled employment. He claimed that jobs were unjustly relocated to low-income foreign countries, and as a result millions of Americans suffered. Finally, according to Trump, successive US administrations were run by incompetent or malicious leaders and administrations. They allowed the USA to enter into bilateral or multilateral agreements which ran counter to US national interests, limiting the country's ability for unilateral action and ruining its economy. Only Trump, he claimed, could save the USA and Make America Great Again. Riding the zeitgeist, Trump surged to power by focusing millions of Americans' concerns with their position in a post–Cold War world where things had not gone to plan: internationally, America was losing its preeminent global role, while at home, the comforting certainties of the past appeared over for many white conservatives, while renewed culture wars roiled the country (Hacker and Pierson, 2005; O'Connell, 2015; Lamb, 2020).

America's political polarisation is characterised by culture wars involving the Christian Right and secular conservatives, on the one hand, and religious and secular liberals, on the other. Many white Christian conservatives, both Protestant and Catholic, agreed with Trump that America was a country where religion, especially Christianity, needed to be protected from secularisation. Many secular white conservatives also liked what they heard when Trump proclaimed he would kick start a new era of American prosperity by strictly controlling immigration and increasing availability of well-paid jobs to native Americans. Trump's neo-nationalism gave his policies focus and direction, appealing to millions of Americans, especially the 73% of the population who in 2017 described themselves as 'white'.[2] Many agreed with Trump that the USA was heading in the wrong direction, both at home and internationally. Only he, they voted, could stop the rot and start a new era of American greatness (Bergmann, 2020: 185–196).

Existential fears: 'uncontrolled' Mexican immigration and 'radical Islamic terrorism'

When Trump assumed the presidency in January 2017, the political, social, and cultural chasm between 'conservatives' and 'liberals' fuelling America's culture wars reached a new peak of intensity. Key issues were the public role of religion, especially religious freedom, children's education, and sexual and gender equality. The USA's culture wars were not new, but Donald Trump successfully exploited them for political gain like no other. He also added another controversial issue to the already fraught political landscape: neo-nationalism.

Donald Trump was elected president amidst rising anti-immigration and 'anti-Muslim' sentiment. According to DiMaggio (2019: 118), Trump's "support for a ban on immigration from Muslim-majority countries, and his plan to build a separation wall between the US and Mexico both demonstrated his support for racist, xenophobic policy positions". Mudde stated that Trump is a nativist because of opportunism rather than belief. Trump quickly learned during the 2016 presidential campaign that

> nativism was *popular*. Trump's campaign speeches were initially quite boring, often with copious allusions to his "always successful" real estate deals, but he noticed that crowds were very pleased when he spoke [about] "building a border wall with Mexico or barring radical Islamic terrorists from the country".
>
> (emphasis in original; Mudde quoted in Freidman, 2017)

Appealing to nativism and fear of the other is not a uniquely Trumpian tactic to acquire votes. García notes that they have been a key characteristic of US politics for at least a century and a half. Initial naturalisation laws in the US allowed only white European immigrants to be eligible for naturalisation. In the mid-19th century, nativists known as the 'Know-Nothings' opposed the entry of German and Irish immigrants into the USA. In 1882, Congress voted to bar Chinese immigration. Nativists also sought to bar from entry into the USA people from Eastern and Southern Europe, including from Russia, Poland, Italy, and Greece. In the early 1920s, immigration was severely limited from those countries via a quota system. In the 1930s, nativists' main fear was unacceptable levels of immigration from Mexico; many blamed Mexicans for the economic woes of the Great Depression, as they were believed to be 'stealing' Americans' jobs. The 1970s saw the invention of a new term, 'illegal alien', which criminalised those attempting to enter the USA illegally. In 1994, California passed Proposition 187 "that denied the undocumented, including their children, access to public services, including education" (García, 2018).

Belew (2018) explains that the development of 'white power' crystallised fears among some Americans about what they saw as whites losing their historical supremacy in a fast-changing country. An upsurge in nativism which saw Trump elected president may have been linked to some voters' feelings of existential insecurity following both 9/11 and the 2008 global financial crisis. Whatever the precise reasons, and no doubt they were varied, millions of Americans agreed with Trump's 'anti-Mexicans' and 'anti-Muslim' rhetoric. The issue, on the one hand, was about illegal immigration into the USA from Mexico and elsewhere in Central America, and, on the other, it targeted both the hundreds of thousands of Muslims living legally in America and those who wanted to immigrate to the USA to improve their life chances. Some Muslims, Trump claimed, actively encouraged or were engaged in terrorist activities (Milton, 2017).

Despite Trump's eye-catching and controversial rhetoric, 91% of voters did not shift their allegiance in 2016, compared to 2012 (McQuarrie, 2017). In other words, in 2016 nine out of ten voters voted for the representative of the same party that they had chosen in 2012. One in ten voters, however, did change their minds. The US electorate was estimated as 253 million in 2018 (Federal Register, 2019). In the 2016 presidential election, an estimated 55.5% of the electorate voted, that is, 138 million of the potential 250 million voters. In 2016, 12.5 million Americans voted differently in 2016 compare to four years earlier. Many among them lived in the so-called Rust Belt states (Illinois, Indiana, Michigan, Ohio, Pennsylvania, and Wisconsin), where large numbers of white working-class voters, traditionally Democrat voters, turned to Trump in 2016.[3] In the Rust Belt states significant numbers of African-Americans, also for the most part long-term Democrat supporters, did not vote in 2016; relatively few voted for Trump (Gaston, 2020: 256–259).

For many among the blue-collar voters of the Rust Belt states, religious issues were not uppermost in their thoughts when they voted in 2016.

What did strike a chord, however, was Trump's emphasis on bread-and-butter issues: jobs and the unwelcome effect on their employment prospects at the thought of 'uncontrolled' immigration from Mexico. These issues were pivotal in attracting blue-collar votes. To explain the shift from the Democratic to the Republican Party in 2016, the economy, especially the availability of jobs, was central. It was the key factor in encouraging significant numbers of voters in the Rust Belt and elsewhere to vote for Trump: 'Making America Great Again' would signify the return of 'American' jobs, and Donald Trump promised that he was the man to make that happen.

Trump and neo-nationalism

> "You know what a globalist is?" Trump said after arguing that Trump was putting America first in opposition to the Democrats who want to "turn back the clock." . . . "A globalist is a person that wants the globe to do well, frankly, not caring about our country so much."
>
> (Koronowski, 2018)

Donald Trump is a neo-nationalist, a populist, and a nativist (Bergmann, 2020). He claims in the previous quotation that he is not a 'globalist'. Why? "And you know what? We can't have that. You know, they have a word. It sort of became old-fashioned. It's called a nationalist" (Koronowski, 2018). Traditionally a secular ideology, nationalism is where an individual identifies with his or her own nation and fundamentally supports its interests, often to the exclusion or detriment of those of other nations. Religious nationalism, on the other hand, understands a nation primarily in religious terms, seeking to further the interests of a particular religious group (Haynes, 2021). Trump combines both secular and religious nationalism, projecting what Bergmann calls "neo-nationalism" (2020).[4] According to Bergmann, neo-nationalism is "nativist populism". It appeals to those who consider themselves the original inhabitants of country. Such people are characterised by both a shared culture and a sense that the fat cats are doing the dirty on them. A nativist believes that the rights of indigenous people are greater than those of immigrants. For some politicians, nativism is appealing during periods when many people feel that harmony between state and nation is declining. For Mudde, nativism is

> xenophobic nationalism . . . an ideology that wants congruence of state and nation – the political and the cultural unit. It wants one state for every nation and one nation for every state. It perceives all

non-natives ... as threatening. But the non-native is not only people. It can also be ideas.

(Mudde quoted in Freidman, 2017)

The attractiveness for some of such dogma is not uniquely American: in the early 2020s, several large and strategically important countries, including India, Russia, and Turkey, were also led by neo-nationalists. Neo-nationalists are values-based politicians. They are against liberalism, globalism, multiculturalism, and cosmopolitanism (Haynes, 2019a: 61–62).

Trump was savvy enough to recognise the political appeal of neo-nationalism and exploit it successfully for electoral gain. His populist and nativist language and policies convinced many millions of Americans to vote for him. Trump's campaign slogan was not new: 'Make America Great Again' was first used by Ronald Reagan at the Republican National Convention in July 1980, when Reagan accepted the Republican Party's presidential nomination.[5] The United States was then undergoing the Iran hostage crisis. At this time, 52 Americans were held by a group of Iranian college students, representatives of the Muslim Student Followers of the Imam's Line, who strongly supported the Iran's Islamic revolution. The students took over the American Embassy in Tehran, holding the Americans captive for 444 days.[6] At the time, the US economy was weak, with both unemployment and price inflation rising. Reagan proclaimed that he would 'Make America Great Again' "for those who've abandoned hope. We'll restore hope and we'll welcome them into a great national crusade to make America great again" ('Ronald Reagan's Commitment to Make America Great Again', 2020).

Ronald Reagan won two presidential elections by successfully exploiting the concerns of Americans who believed that the days of the country's greatness were gone and should be restored. Reagan, like Trump four decades later, was also successful in tapping into fears of the then burgeoning Christian Right that America was secularising; regarded as very bad news for the religious freedom of tens of millions of Christian conservatives who thought the secularist socialists were coming for them. Reagan also spoke to many less-religious and secular American conservatives, especially the many who believed that they were missing out economically as previously secure and relatively well-paid jobs diminished. Like Trump, four decades later, Reagan rode a wave of popular discontent, especially among white working-class men, to electoral victory (O'Connell, 2015: 50–77).

Like presidential elections in the 1980s, Trump's victory occurred during a deepening of the country's culture wars. For Jacoby (2014), there is "strong evidence that there is a culture war generating fundamental divisions within twenty-first century American society". As in the 1980s, America's culture wars three decades later significantly undermined the country's political, social, cultural, and economic unity. Over time, the foci of the culture wars have remained constant: mainly white Christian nationalists against secular and religious liberals, concerned about a 'woman's right to choose'/'killing a baby', Christian prayers in schools, and religious freedom. Like Reagan, Trump claimed he was the only person who would aggressively defend Christians against godless secularists who, he thundered, wanted to eliminate America's constitutionally derived religious freedoms. This was a key factor encouraging many practising Christians, especially white Protestant conservatives and white Catholic conservatives, to vote for Trump. He especially built his appeal among existing or new Republican voters, an estimated 80% of whom were white conservative Christians in 2016 (Fea, 2018). Many did not regard Donald Trump as an exemplary Christian; far from it. Instead, as Sides, Tesler, and Vavreck note (2019), many were highly alarmed by America's "identity crisis, concerns that Trump successfully exploited to win enough votes, via the vagaries of the Electoral College system, to enter the White House". What explains the white Christian conservative embrace of Trump?[7] Fea (2018) asserts that it was a logical outcome of a long-standing approach to public life characterised by the politics of fear, the pursuit of worldly power, and a nostalgic longing for an American past, when such people ruled America and everyone knew their societal, economic, and political place. In addition, Sides, Tesler, and Vavreck (2019) point to Trump's 'partisan manipulation', explicit appeals and rhetoric aimed at religious and secular conservatives. Whether the issue was 'Build That Wall' to keep out 'Mexicans' or to protect America's Christian heritage from attacks by 'secularists', conservatives were strongly behind Trump in 2016. Many, but not all, retained their support for him as the 2020 presidential election approached, even though many Americans blamed the Trump administration's inadequate response to the coronavirus pandemic for the more than 230,000 deaths as a direct result of contracting Covid-19 that Americans had endured by voting day: 3 November 2020.[8]

In the next section of the chapter, I identify the defining characteristics of two groups of Trump voters: Christian nationalists and what I refer to as 'America First' nationalists. Christian nationalism is a political ideology associated with America's Christian Right, a powerful political movement which dominates the Republican Party, having grown in strength since the 1980s. America First nationalism, on the other hand, is a secular ideology informed by an understanding that the USA's well-being, security, and stability is under prolonged attack by liberals and socialists at home and foreigners abroad. The basic difference between the two is their adhesion to religion: Christian nationalists believe that to make America great again it is necessary to pursue policies with appropriately Christian conservative characteristics. It requires Christian education in schools and, during the coronavirus pandemic, the ability to worship without government interference. Overall, it means a Christianised America with laws tied to what Christian conservatives demand. America First nationalists, on the other hand, are primarily concerned with bread-and-butter issues at home, including jobs and immigration, and the USA's national interests abroad, putting 'America First'. Separating out the two groups in this way is however a heuristic device, seeking to aid understanding of specific social phenomena. It inevitably involves use of an artificial construct, based on assumptions originating from extant empirical research, linked to identification of ideal types in order to define their characteristics. The overall aim is to set out the salient features of Christian nationalists and America First nationalists as clearly and as explicitly as possible, while being aware of the limitations of such a preliminary analysis regarding these complex social phenomena.

Christian nationalism and America First nationalism

Christian nationalism

Nationalism is a powerful marker of individual identity. Much of the early work done in studies of nationalism had foundations, often implicitly, in the idea that religion, a traditional genealogical carrier of identity, was largely replaced during modernisation by a secular ideology: nationalism. 'National identity' and its ideological manifestation, nationalism, emerged to fill a void as Western countries modernised and secularised, significantly undermining religion's public prominence.

America was not, however, among those Western countries which obviously saw a public decline of religion. In 1954, in response to the threat from the Soviet Union, President Eisenhower encouraged Congress to add the words 'under God', creating the current 31-word pledge of allegiance. The Establishment Clause of the First Amendment of the US constitution states that the government must remain neutral in religious matters. Adding 'under God' to the pledge underlined that American governments endorse religion as a highly desirable, although not obligatory, societal characteristic. It was possible to pledge loyalty to the flag and country without necessarily having to identify with America's majority religion: Christianity.

Many scholars now question the claim that religion and nationalism are necessarily separate. This is because of the apparent persistence or growth of religious identities in many countries around the world, both 'developed' and 'underdeveloped', which are also characterised as nationalist, including India, Russia, and Turkey. Sometimes, as significant aspects of self-identification, they might be in tension, such as in Israel where the religious character of the state is questioned by many secular and liberal Israelis. Or, they act in mutually supportive ways, as in America during the era of 'civil religion' until the mid-1960s, when the Vietnam War indicated a societal polarisation which also involved religious Americans. Rogers Brubaker (2017) has recently put forward 'views' or 'strategies' to explain the relationship between religion and nationalism. Others, including J. Christopher Soper and Joel Fetzer (2018), depict their relationship as a continuum. Ideal-type 'secular nationalism' is at one end and a fully realised 'religious nationalism' is at the other. Somewhere in the middle of the continuum is 'civil-religious nationalism', for several decades understood to be the situation in America, with characteristics of both (Metzner, 2020).

This is not to imply that the pledge of allegiance with its 'under God' refrain reflects Christian nationalism's dominant social or political role in America today. It does, however, indicate that America is a country where both Christianity and nationalism may go hand in hand, as fundamental aspects of American culture, and today this is manifested for some as Christian nationalism. Trump's coming to power relied on his ability to gain the votes of most white Christian conservatives, both Protestant and Catholic. In this book, I am categorising white Christian conservatives as 'Christian nationalists'. However, there is a growing literature on Christian nationalism and a lack of consensus about what the term means. I understand a white Christian nationalist in the USA as a nativist American who believes it necessary for America to return to the country's religious roots, whose foundations are a more 'Christian' and 'nationalist' America, strongly supportive of religious – especially Christian – freedom at home and abroad. Many white Christian conservatives who voted for Trump believe that the USA is being undermined by 'alien' religions and cultures (especially Islam) and by anti-religion liberals and socialists actively encouraging secularisation in order to arrive at a secular country (Holpuch, 2019).

The US-based Institute of Social Policy and Understanding commissioned a poll of 2,481 Americans in early 2018. It found that "white [Christian] Evangelicals" expressed "the highest levels of Islamophobia"[9] among seven identified groups, some faith-based, some not (ISPU, 2018). Forty per cent of "white Evangelicals" agreed that "most Muslims living in the United States" are "more prone to violence than other people", are "hostile to the United States", are "less civilized than other people", are "partially responsible for acts of violence carried out by other Muslims" and "discriminate against women".[10] In other words, four in ten white Evangelicals in the USA believe Muslims are uncivilised, violent, against the USA, and misogynist. A recent Pew Research Center (2018) study on "Religion in public life" indicates that one-quarter (25.4%) of Americans identify themselves as Evangelicals, that is, around 80 million people. Of these, three-quarters

(76%) are white. Thus, extrapolating from the data in the aforementioned 2018 survey, around 60 million Americans are "white Evangelicals". If 40% see America's Muslims as uncivilised, violent, against the USA, and misogynist, it implies that around 24 million white Evangelicals in the USA share such beliefs. In addition, according to the 2018 Pew poll, 31% of Protestants and 22% of Catholics hold such views. In the 2016 presidential elections, 81% of white Evangelicals, 60% of "white Catholics" and 58% of "Protestants/other Christians" voted for Trump, while, respectively, 39% and 37% voted for Clinton (Pew Research Centre, 2016).

According to the Pew Research Center, most Americans know extremely little about Islam and personally know very few if any Muslims; Muslims are thin on the ground in the USA: about 1% of the country's overall population, or 3.5 million people (Pew Research Center, 2017). This is the context in which Donald Trump successfully exploited many Americans' concerns about a perceived "Islamic threat", especially from "radical Islamic terrorism" and sharia law. Finally, a 2017 Pew Research Center Report indicated that Republicans are more fearful of Muslims than are Democrats.

Quoting the Austrian author Kurt Seinitz, Kamali (2015: 204) notes that for all the talk of globalisation bringing increased diversity, many Westerners, including Americans, continue to demonstrate a widespread lack of basic knowledge about Islam. That deficiency is compounded in the USA, as elsewhere in the West, by social secularisation and accompanying death of religious taboos, which serves to decrease interest in and empathy with non-Western religions. This helps explain how right-wing populist politicians in the USA and other Western countries are successful electorally by pointing to a perceived or imagined existential threat from 'Islam' and Muslims, especially 'radical Islamic terrorism', to justify draconian, anti-Muslim policies in the interests of 'security'. Examples of such a policy include President Trump's executive order barring from entry into the USA people from six or seven mainly Muslim countries, from which no one had ever been convicted of terrorism in America (Adida, Laitin, and Valfort, 2016).

We shall see in a later chapter that another key concern for Christian nationalists is religious freedom: the freedom to practise religion, unconstrained by the state. This, together with the fear of Islam, briefly noted earlier, are the two defining characteristics of Christian nationalism in America.

America First nationalism

America First nationalism has a long history, dating back to the 1930s ('Can American Nationalism Be Saved?', 2019; Lowry, 2019; Miller, 2020). In the 2020s, America First nationalists are concerned with immigration and jobs at home. Internationally, they want to see the USA recover its formerly pre-eminent position by refocusing away from internationalist commitments to American national interest policies. Donald Trump has expressed his disdain and apprehension of 'globalism'. Like Trump, America First nationalists believe that globalism implies the 'export' of American jobs to foreign countries where wages are cheaper, for the benefit of 'fat cat' capitalists, not American workers.

Donald Trump was able to attract a high level of electoral support, including from among the United States' 'dispossessed'. These are mainly un- or under-employed white men in low-level, unskilled, or semi-skilled jobs, mostly lacking a college education, who saw their current positions and future prospects diminish as a result of both the effects of economic globalisation ('exporting American jobs') and large numbers of sometimes illegal immigrants from Mexico and elsewhere who were prepared to work for less in diminished conditions (Jackson, 2016).

President Trump is a self-proclaimed 'America First' nationalist. Like Donald Trump, America First nationalists want to bolster the USA's sovereignty at home and abroad. President Trump wants to 'Make American Great Again' by curtailing immigration from Central America and from several Muslim countries in order to advance the position of nativist Americans, both culturally and in terms of employment. America First nationalism was to the fore when Trump swiftly put into effect an election promise to curtail illegal immigration. The policy was aimed primarily at people from named Muslim-majority countries and illegal 'Mexican' immigrants, vilified by Trump as rapists and criminals, from entering the country (Haynes, 2019a). Promising to build a 'big, beautiful' wall to keep out illegal immigrants, Trump made the issue of central concern during the 2016 presidential election campaign, including in televised political debates between presidential candidates. The focus, on the one hand, was on illegal immigration into the USA from Mexico and Central America and, on the other hand, there was the question of some immigrants' loyalty to the USA. Trump and several other Republican candidates, such as Ted Cruz, openly questioned the loyalties of America's more than three million Muslims. Both issues centre on whether specific groups of people – that is, 'Mexicans' and Muslims – are to be fully trusted by nativist Americans. Do the former demonstrate 'sufficient' and 'acceptable' levels of national loyalty to, commitment to, and identity with the USA? In other words, are they nationalist enough?

America First nationalism concerns as expressed by President Trump were not novel in 2016, as seen in the following quotation from 1998, extracted from a book by the current author:

> In the late 1990s it seems to many observers that America is a country torn by economic, political and cultural insecurities. Angry white

12 *Introduction*

> people blame African-Americans and immigrants for taking their jobs. Unemployed African-Americans look to blame the Hispanics. Forty million Americans have no health insurance, while blue-collar wages have fallen by nearly 20 per cent in real terms since the 1970s. Middle management is regularly 'downsized', while manufacturing jobs relocate to low-wage countries in Asia and Latin America. Meanwhile, the richest 2 per cent of the population control the majority of the wealth. A single company, communications giant AT&T, shed 40,000 jobs in the mid-1990s, while its chief executive enjoyed a $5 million (£3.2 million) rise in the value of his share options. In short, the USA is racked by scapegoating and chronic insecurity.
>
> (Haynes, 1998: 223–224)

The issues which animated America First nationalists a quarter of a century ago are the same as those that Trump more recently was able to exploit for electoral gain. In the 1990s, the end of the Cold War and subsequent international turmoil were instrumental in ushering in economic, cultural, and social changes which affected deleteriously many Americans' perception of their country's security, stability, and well-being. This was not, of course, unique to the USA; similar effects were felt around the world. But each country experiences such changes differently, linked to their domestic political and cultural histories. In the 1990s, America was already engaged in culture wars, pitting Christian conservatives against liberals and secularists. Add to this the impact of globalisation and associated international changes, and it is easy to see why America First nationalism finds a receptive audience among many Americans, especially among those on the 'sharp end' of the resultant changes.

For Trump and America First nationalists more generally, economic globalisation signifies something bad: 'globalism'. It reflects an increasingly interdependent global economy. On the other hand, globalisation undermines national sovereignty, diminishing states' capacities to pursue successfully independent macroeconomic and development strategies and policies (Haynes, 2005b). Economic globalisation has both widened and deepened since the 1990s, a phase of world history characterised by a recent culmination of European colonial rule, diminution of the USA's hitherto dominant economic position, fragmentation and collapse of the Soviet Union, and exponential growth in the internationalisation of productive capital and finance. Together, these four developments have resulted in both disruption and destabilisation, affecting even large powerful industrialised states such as the USA, which, as a result, has declining options in relation to economic, including welfare, policies. Today, all states – rich and poor, weak and strong, large and small – are exposed to networks of economic forces and relations that range both in and through them. This reduces all states' ability to pursue autonomous economic and developmental policies, including in relation to international migration. It is such developments that Donald Trump pledged to fight against during his 2016 election campaign. He promised to use America's global power to transform the extant international order, based since World War II on cooperation and internationally consensual goals and expressed through the United Nations, into an environment dominated by states' national interest concerns, not those of the international community.

As a result of economic globalisation, states' monetary and fiscal policies had to take cognisance of the influence of globally orientated economic migrants, including millions of people who at any one time are actively seeking to migrate from a less-favoured territory to another where they believe their prospects and life chances, and those of their children, will be significantly improved. This provides an important component of the 'pull' factor, encouraging people from relatively near yet less economically favoured countries, such as Mexico and many Central American countries, to attempt to reach the USA to improve their life chances and those of their children. Trump's election and political successes of neo-nationalists elsewhere at the current time reflect a widespread backlash against immigration in the USA and many European countries.

According to Moran, Trump's foreign policy is 'Jacksonian'. This is a reference to an earlier nationalist president, Andrew Jackson (1829–1837). Like Jackson, Trump effectively exploited nationalist concerns for political gain (Moran, 2021: 367). Walter Russell Mead (2017) argues that Jacksonians like Trump see the government's main key priority as taking care of "the physical security and economic well-being of the American people in their national home". Trump gives short shrift to the concerns of 'globalists' who 'want the globe to do well'. The implication is that it is a zero-sum game: if my country does well the globe does badly; if the globe does well, my country suffers. The Trump administration's perception of international agreements seems to be that unless they primarily benefit America's national priorities, they cannot be beneficial to the USA.

For America First nationalists, the culture wars at home were about ethnic and cultural diversity informed by an understanding that globalisation seriously threatens America's prosperity and well-being. America First nationalists are 'anti-globalists', that is, they are suspicious and fearful of globalisation because it has led to a reduction in America's potential prosperity. Globalisation needs to be fought against in order to maximise America's well-being. America First nationalists also feel threatened by America's growing ethnic and cultural diversity, which has been gaining pace since the Immigration and Naturalization Act of 1965 (also known as the Hart-Celler

Act). The act abolished an earlier quota system based on national origin. It established a new immigration policy based on reuniting immigrant families and attracting skilled labour to the United States.

The distrust of America First anti-globalists also feeds off the 'clash of civilisations' thesis, advanced by the late American political scientist Samuel Huntington (1993, 1996). Huntington saw two main threats to the wellbeing of America, racial dilution at home and international threats from China and Islam (Hayes, 2019). Globalisation makes international interactions inevitable, and Huntington believed that the values, beliefs, and behaviour of China and Islam were different from that of the USA, which were moulded by European-style Protestant Christianity. Cooperation was impossible and conflict highly likely.[11] Huntington's last book, *Who Are We? The Challenges to America's National Identity* (2004) examined the USA in relation to racial diversity. Huntington claimed that America's peace and prosperity had their foundations in Christian cultural foundations brought from Europe. For Huntington, 'diluting' it with recent non-Protestant immigrants, such as Catholic Mexicans and Muslims, fatally undermined America's capacity to be a 'melting pot', that is, to incorporate numerous cultures and ways of like without excessive strife in the 150 years following the end in 1865 of America's civil war.

Like Christian conservatives, many blue-collar former Democrat voters in the Rust Belt states saw Trump as the leader to arrest America's decline (Smith, 2017). Christian conservatives believed Trump would reverse what they saw as a calamitous turning away from America's Christian foundations. America First nationalists voted for Trump out of concern at what they saw as a dramatic reduction in of American prestige and international standing. For both groups, Trump was the 'Alpha male', the strong leader to 'make America great again'.

The methodology and structure of the book

Before going further, a few words on methodology. The current book employs a qualitative methodology. It is informed by 82 mainly face-to-face interviews conducted personally by the author with individuals with knowledge of issues germane to the volume. The interviews took place mainly between 2015 and 2018 in the USA and in various European countries (Belgium, France, Germany, Italy, Norway, Poland, and the United Kingdom). Bolstering the interviews, research for the book was undertaken mainly via internet research. It involved archive investigations which yielded relevant primary and secondary source documents, including US government documents. Internet research was especially necessary from March 2020 as the Covid-19 pandemic eviscerated the chances of doing research via fieldwork in the USA.

Introduction 15

The starting point for research for the current book was a three-year research programme (2015–2017) conducted under the auspices of the Enhancing Life Project (ELP), led by Professor Bill Schweiker (University of Chicago, USA) and Professor Gunther Thomas (Ruhr-University Bochum, Germany), supported by a generous grant from the John Templeton Foundation (http://enhancinglife.uchicago.edu/). The author of the current book was one of the 35 scholars involved in the ELP, working on a project entitled: 'The United Nations Alliance of Civilizations: an Effective Actor to Improve Global Dialogue?' The results of my research on the ELP project were published in Haynes (2018, 2019a, etc.).

Following the end of the ELP research project in August 2017, I decided to augment that study with a wider geographical focus to include not only the United Nations in New York, but also the then newly inaugurated administration of Donald Trump in the contemporaneous context of surging neo-nationalism in Europe. Samuel Huntington's 'clash of civilizations' paradigm was a common theme in each of the three contexts – the United Nations, the USA, and Europe. To pursue the theme of the impact of the 'clash of civilizations' on international, regional, and national contexts, including in the USA, further interviews were undertaken in Washington DC in April 2018 and in the same year in several European countries, including the UK and Poland and at the European Union. Early results of the research were published in Haynes (2019a, 2019b). This book focuses on the USA, using insights gleaned from the wider research programme I undertook since 2015.

The rest of this introductory chapter explains the structure of the book, briefly describing each of the constituent chapters.

Chapter 1, entitled 'From Nationalism to Neo-nationalism', examines development of nationalism as a secular ideology from the 19th century, explaining how it developed into neo-nationalism combining religious, cultural, civilisational, and secular concerns. In Europe, neo-nationalism tends to be cultural rather than religious, related to the advanced regional state of secularisation. In the USA, on the other hand, neo-nationalism is buoyed by Christian nationalism and America First nationalism. Both categories primarily involve white American conservatives, the main adherents to neo-nationalism in the USA.

The chapter explains America's political polarisation during the Trump administration, fuelled by an exponential growth of partisanship, which feeds into both Christian and America First nationalism, on the one hand, and into the liberal view, on the other. The Christian Right/Republican Party is engaged in culture wars with secularists, the LGBTQ community, feminists, and religious liberals. In sum, the chapter traces the causes and effects of nationalism evolving into neo-nationalism in America.

The second chapter – 'Culture Wars and Neo-nationalism' – surveys America's 'culture wars' from the Reagan presidency in the 1980s and examines their influence on neo-nationalism in the Trump presidency. Chapter 3 is titled 'Neo-nationalism and Politics in the USA'. It examines domestic neo-nationalist policies during the Trump presidency. The chapter examines Christian nationalist policies – including Project Blitz and attempts at state-level anti-abortion measures – and America First nationalist policies – including anti-immigration efforts from Mexico and selected Muslim-majority countries. The main goal of America's Christian nationalists is to increase religious freedom and to decrease the state's influence. Critics claim that this is primarily about protecting Christians, although it is acknowledged that some other religious groups – such as China's Uighurs – also receive the support of the USA (Marsden, 2020). Advancing international religious freedom was a key goal of American foreign policy during the Trump presidency. It was not, however, a new goal. International religious freedom has been a formal goal of US foreign policy since the 1998 passing of the International Religious Freedom (IRF) Act, signed into law by President Bill Clinton (Haynes, 2008; Bettiza, 2019). During the first decade of the 21st century, presidents Bush and Obama pursued IRF policies with "an implicit Christian soft spot". The Trump administration took this further, prioritising "attention to Christian concerns and communities" which became "even more overt and explicit", compared to the Bush and Obama presidencies (Bettiza, 2019: 223). For the Trump administration, international religious freedom was not 'just' about the freedom to pursue your chosen religion. It was also ideological, favouring Christian nationalist goals, such as anti-abortion and against gender and LGBTQ equality. Trump's favouring of Christian nationalist goals was a direct response to his popularity among this constituency, especially among white conservative Christians (Haynes, 2020a).

Chapter 4 – 'Neo-nationalism and America's International Relations' – argues that, in line with the president's neo-nationalism which combines the preferences of America First and Christian nationalists, US international relations reflects aspects of the country's culture wars. Two facets of the culture wars are most salient: (1) elimination of US support for the institutions of the post–World War II liberal international order, especially the United Nations and (2) US attempts to rewrite post–World War II international conventions on human rights in line with Christian nationalist preferences. This is expressed in the relinquishment of US support for the universalist post–World War international human rights regime, as expressed in the Universal Declaration of Human Rights (1948), and replacement by a particularistic policy, moulded by Christian nationalism, to champion international religious freedom as the paramount human right.

In addition, the Trump presidency no longer sought to pursue America's longstanding international role as 'leader of the free world'. This involved two foci: international cooperation, especially at the United Nations, to spread and disseminate America's proclaimed core values: democracy, religious freedom, and trouble-free international trade. Trump came to power promising to 'make America great again', enlisting the support of both Christian and less-religious nationalists. Domestically, Christian nationalists identify themselves as patriots and want to see the USA return to its roots: both more 'Christian' and more 'nationalist', that is, concerned primarily with America rather than seeking to right global wrongs. They strongly supported Trump's policies which, inter alia, sought to undermine in the USA what the president presented as 'alien' religions (especially Islam) and internationally to favour the USA and undermine the influence of international organisations, such as the United Nations. Secular nationalists focus primarily on the global position of the USA, especially in terms of America's trading position vis-à-vis China, Iran, Mexico, and the European Union.

Chapter 5 is the concluding chapter. It summarises the arguments of the book's individual's chapters. It concludes by emphasising that the Trump phenomenon has been building for decades, and the Trump presidency used the impact of significant political, social, economic, and cultural disquiet at home to fashion and progress policies which appealed in particular to many Christian nationalists and America First nationalists. The chapter is followed by a brief epilogue which discusses the end of Trump's presidency and prospects for the future of America during the tenure of President Biden.

Notes

1 A canard endorsed and spread by Trump.
2 "White people constitute the majority of the U.S. population, with a total of about 234,370,202 or 73% of the population as of 2017" (https://en.wikipedia.org/wiki/Demographics_of_the_United_States)
3 In 2018, the size of the electorate in the six 'Rust Belt' states was: Illinois, 9,883,814; Indiana, 5,123,748; Michigan, 7,831,247; Ohio, 9,096,117; Pennsylvania, 10,158,149; Wisconsin, 4,537,465. The overall total of potential voters in the six states was 46,630,540, that is, 18% of the total US electorate of just over 250 million (Federal Register, 2019).
4 The title of the current book was inspired by Eirikur Bergmann's (2020) recent analyst of the global spread of neo-nationalism.
5 Ronald Reagan was the first US presidential candidate to employ the slogan 'Let's Make America Great Again' during the 1980 presidential election campaign.
6 The Americans were both diplomats and 'ordinary' citizens. They were held hostage from November 4, 1979, to January 20, 1981.

18 *Introduction*

7 Christian evangelicals are divided; the National Association of Evangelicals is a notable critic of Trump, especially over his alleged moral deficiencies and his hostility towards some immigration.
8 To put the 230,000 coronavirus deaths in America in nine months in 2020 into perspective, an estimated 47,424 American soldiers died in the two-decades-long Vietnam War (1955–75). In World War II, 291,557 US service personnel were killed. During nine months of the coronavirus pandemic in 2020, America experienced 75% of the numbers of deaths of US soldiers in World War II, a conflict which for the USA lasted nearly four years (8 December 1941–2 September 1945).
9 A much-cited Runnymede Trust publication defines Islamophobia as "a useful shorthand way of referring to dread or hatred of Islam" (Runnymede Trust, 1997: 1).
10 The poll measured 'Islamophobia' on a scale of 0 to 100, with 100 the highest. In addition to 'white Evangelicals', other groups scored as follows: Protestants, 31%; 'General Public', 24%; Jewish, 22%; Catholics, 22%; Muslims, 14%; and 'Non-affiliated', 14%.
11 During the Reagan presidency, the 'clash of civilisations' theme was different: 'Christian' America against the 'godless' Soviet Union.

1 From nationalism to neo-nationalism

The Trump presidency is characterised by political polarisation and partisanship, which feed its ideology of neo-nationalism. Drawing on both Christian nationalism and secular nationalism, the Trump administration's neo-nationalism is not altogether new. It is reminiscent of the ideology of the presidency of Ronald Reagan (1981–1989) who also thrived on political division between conservatives and liberals (Wiebe, 2002). The eight years of the Reagan presidency in the 1980s occurred during a period of major social and political changes, both at home and abroad. At home, the decade saw the political rise of the Christian Right. Internationally, America's culture wars with the Soviet Union came to a head in the 1980s, a decade which saw the fall of the Berlin Wall, followed in 1991 by the collapse of the USSR.

Following the Reagan presidency, the Christian Right came to dominate the Republican Party. In the early 2020s, the Christian Right/Republican Party was on one side of America's culture wars. On the other side were religious liberals and secularists, as well as many in the LGBTQ community, greens, and feminists. To understand today's culture wars in the USA, it is useful to trace the rise of neo-nationalism in America. This we do in the current chapter. We examine the USA's culture wars in more detail in Chapter 2.

The chapter begins by tracing the emergence and development of nationalism, a secular ideology, in the 19th century. This was a time when European nations sought to make themselves great via colonialism. Later, nationalism fell from favour, inextricably linked to the hyper-nationalisms of Nazi Germany, Mussolini-era Italy, and Japan during the reign of Emperor Hirohito. The chapter explains that in the decades after World War II, conflictual nationalisms re-emerged, for example, in the civil wars of former Yugoslavia in the 1990s. Over time, nationalism developed into neo-nationalism, which combines religious, cultural, and secular concerns. Finally, the chapter explains that neo-nationalism is not the same everywhere: for example, in Europe neo-nationalism is often culturally rather than religiously focused, because of the advanced state of secularisation in most regional countries. On the other hand, in the USA during the Trump presidency, neo-nationalism was fuelled by both Christian nationalism and America First nationalism.

Emergence and development of nationalism

Europeans created an 'international society' in the 19th and 20th centuries (Haynes, Hough, Malik, and Pettiford, 2017: 20–36). Consequential to acquisition of extensive foreign territories, European powers, notably the French and British, sought to spread their political institutions and values via colonialism and imperialism. Their stated aim was to spread their 'civilisation' by undermining 'barbarism' and teaching 'savages' how to be 'civilised'. Many Europeans believed that such international society-building activities were not only legitimate but also necessary to enable power balancing, following a long period of nationalist turmoil in Europe in the 18th and 19th centuries. These efforts were rarely welcomed by emerging national elites in Africa, Asia, and elsewhere after World War I and particularly following World War II. The European powers were especially weakened by the latter conflict. Decolonisation after World War II was a crucial component in the globalisation of nationalism, as dozens of post-colonial countries sought to build a sense of national identity in newly independent states. Lind explains that after the Cold War, it was very widely agreed in

> the North Atlantic democracies that there was a new struggle between . . . enlightened, progressive forces of internationalism – symbolized by the global market and/or supranational regional blocs like the European Union – and nationalists . . . dismissed contemptuously as racists, xenophobes, and protectionists who failed to understand economics.
>
> (Lind, 2001)

Lind is highlighting the main differences between 'nationalism' and 'internationalism', which became especially apparent after the Cold War and the demise of the Soviet Union. As he notes, nationalists were typically regarded by liberals and 'progressives' as regressive, out of sync with the internationally orientated North Atlantic democracies and their pursuit of universal goals, including democracy and human rights. "'In most elite circles", he claims, "one who had anything favourable to say about nationalism met with suspicion or contempt" (Lind, 2001). For such people, internationalism was widely believed to be the way of the future, crucial for the development of a progressive and cooperative 'new world order' led by the liberal democracies of the North Atlantic region. Internationalists regarded nationalism as decidedly old hat: the way of the past. It was seen as insular, backward looking, and unsuited for the challenges of the post–Cold War world. Internationalism was the way of the future.

Despite their distaste, internationalists would find it hard to disagree that historically nationalism has been a potent force, both nationally and internationally. Nationalism is variously interpreted as ideology or political movement.[1] I understand a 'political ideology' to comprise an entity's ethical ideals, principles, doctrines, myths, and/or symbols. They are used both to explain how society should work and to offer a political and cultural plan for a desirable social order. The ideology of nationalism asserts that a nation has the political right to constitute itself as an independent, sovereign political community, because of both a perceived shared history and a common destiny. As a political movement, a nation is a group of people of indeterminate but normally considerable size often but not always living in the same country, who believe themselves distinctive and unique, manifested by community ties that are both significant and persistent. When forming a political movement, nationalists believe that it is only right and proper that state borders should dovetail, as precisely as possible, with a nation's boundaries. In extreme cases, such as that demonstrated in the extremist ideology of Nazi Germany, the state regards the nation as *the* supreme facet of a person's identity, superior to all other relevant attributes, such as religion, class, race, and gender.

Some scholars of nationalism, such as Walker Connor (1994) and Anthony D. Smith (1972), assert that national sentiment has both deep roots and persistent power. Others, such as Elie Kedourie (1993) and Eric Hobsbawm (2021), predict that nationalism is destined to fade away, replaced by internationalism. For Hobsbawm, nationalism is a kind of false consciousness. He believes that nationalist sentiments that arose among different ethnic groups in Europe in the 19th century, later extending to much of the rest of the world via colonialism, were not authentic popular movements. Instead, they were the result of elites' effective propaganda. They wanted to create new states and, often, to lead them. The elite strategy to create cohesive nation-states out of fragmenting empires was to persuade members of their own ethnic group into believing in the existence of a historic 'nation', even when they had not necessarily thought of themselves in that way before.

Wiebe (2002) expresses a different view. He argues that the rise of nationalism in the 19th century was a sensible human adaptation to the travails of modernisation. During that phase of development, people moved in great numbers from small to large population centres. Under the circumstances, it seemed logical and natural for them to rely on family, kin, and/or ethnic and religious networks to aid them in their brave new world, with, for example, news, jobs, and money. Wiebe contends that these networks of trust and affection grew both demographically and geographically, to encompass not only people from one's home community but also from one's region and, eventually, to all those who spoke the same language. From there, he suggests, it is a short step to nationalism. For Wiebe, "[e]thnicity turned into nationalism when cultural consciousness acquired a political objective, such as the aspiration for self-government or removal of oppression". As a result, "[e]thnicity and nationalism . . . solved problems migration posed" (Lind, 2001).

Secular nationalism and religious nationalism

The nation-building process in post-colonial states continued during the Cold War. Some sought to develop by linking ideologically, diplomatically, militarily, and financially with one of the superpowers, either the USA or the Soviet Union. These relationships, however, were fundamentally thrown into question by the fall of the Berlin Wall in November 1989 and the sudden demise of the USSR in December 1991. It appeared to many that the Cold War would be followed by the universal triumph of Western-style liberal democracy and capitalism, presaging a new cooperative phase of international relations: a new world order based on 'Western values' with increasing, maybe universal, legitimacy. In the mid-1990s, however, it became clear that a newly cooperative new world order based on the spread of perceived Western values was not occurring; instead, a new world *dis*order was developing, marked by serious clashes of nationalisms in several countries, notably former Yugoslavia and Ethiopia. A decade later, the events of 11 September 2001 ('9/11') emphatically ended the brief period of internationalist liberal utopianism. It was followed by a Manichaean struggle between the forces of what some refer to as 'enlightened globalisation' – represented by, for example, multinational corporations and nongovernmental organisations – and 'anti-globalists', whom progressives regard as advocates of self-interested 'reactionary' nationalism, including Donald Trump, Viktor Orbán, and Narendra Modi, as well as the transnational religious fundamentalisms of al-Qaeda and the Islamic State (Haynes, 2005a, 2019a).

In addition, 9/11 highlighted the often-close relationship of religion to secular nationalism. This was clear, for example, within the Arab Muslim world, "especially where", as Wiebe (2002) notes, "shallow-rooted, kleptocratic states presided over impoverished Moslem populations". The appeal of Osama bin Laden's brand of Islamist extremism owed a great deal to the failure of Nasser's secular pan-Arabism (Haynes, 2005b). More widely, the post-9/11 world highlighted the unclear relationship between religion and secular nationalism. Some renowned scholars of nationalism, including Ernest Gellner (1983) and Eric Hobsbawm (2021), do not include religion when discussing nationalism. Instead, they highlight in the growth of nationalism the importance of various secular – that is, historical and economic – factors. It is now however widely recognised following the civil war in former Yugoslavia, 9/11, and the Arab Spring events that to develop a comprehensive understanding of nationalism, it is necessary to factor in religion's direct and indirect influences (Reiffer, 2003).

Anthony D. Smith is comparatively rare among scholars of nationalism in that he discusses in depth the relationship between religion and (secular) nationalism. Smith claims, "perhaps more detrimental than anything to our understanding of these phenomena has been the general trend to dismiss the role of religion and tradition in a globalizing world, and to downplay the persistence of nationalism in a 'post-national' global order" (Smith, 2003: ix). In relation to the USA, for example, it is impossible to understand American nationalism both historically and today without considering formative Christian – primarily, mainline Protestant – beliefs and values (Green, Rozell, and Wilcox, 2003).

'Religious nationalism' refers to a close or synonymous relationship between religion and nationalism. It is an important component of present-day international life, because today many nations define themselves at least in part in terms of their 'national' religious beliefs, which are frequently connected to related components of identity, such as culture, race, ethnicity, and language. Some countries have a state ideology of religious nationalism, for example, Iran, Saudi Arabia, Afghanistan (under the rule of the Taliban [1996–2001]) and perhaps Russia under Putin, where the state and the Orthodox Church have a symbiotic relationship. When a regime seeks to derive its political legitimacy primarily from public adherence to religious, not secular, doctrines, then we have a theocracy: that is, a state dominated by those who believe themselves, or are widely thought to be, divinely guided. This is the case in both Saudi Arabia and Iran. Beyond these countries, Reiffer notes several ways that religion and nationalism typically interact, albeit with varying degrees of influence. Whereas religious nationalism in Iran and Saudi Arabia refers axiomatically to an inseparable relationship between religion and nationalism, many other nationalist expressions also draw on religious beliefs, without necessarily playing a pivotal role: this is when religion "assist[s] the more prominent nationalist movement as a cohesive element" (Reiffer, 2003: 215). Many extant examples of such a relationship between religion and nationalism can be noted, especially in the Global South, including in Sri Lanka, India, Pakistan, and Tibet. In these countries and territories, religion and culture are important markers of group identity. They are not necessarily a fundamental driver of nationalist political claims; that is, religion does not inevitably occupy a central position in the nationalist movement. The primary concern is the political goal of achieving or consolidating a nation-state which, if achieved, is likely to draw importantly on religion and culture as significant ideological components of wider nationalist aspirations.

Some religious nationalists want to do away with the secular state and replace it with one whose values, beliefs, rituals, and processes emanate from their religious beliefs. Juergensmeyer argues that this is when the secular state is regarded not only as both dysfunctional and morally and spiritually bankrupt. For many, however, such a religious state would be inherently 'anti-modern', because both legitimacy and authority of the state would be based on traditional religious principles, not modern secular principles. Juergensmeyer (2005) contends that religious nationalism is likely to continue to expand both geographically and in terms of its influence, especially but not only in the Global South. The target of some religious nationalists in the Global South would likely be the West in general or individual Western governments in particular, as shown by the events of 9/11 and assorted terrorist outrages over time in several Western countries. To counteract these actors, Juergensmeyer argues that Western governments need to adopt a strategy of cooperation, not confrontation, with religious nationalists. Thus, to counter religious nationalists of al-Qaeda and ISIS it makes sense for their target – the USA and the West more generally – to work cooperatively against them. More generally, the examples of al-Qaeda and ISIS highlight that while religion can make essential contributions to human development it can also have a strongly malign influence. On the plus side, religion can help people by (1) giving life greater metaphysical meaning and hope of improved well-being, (2) moulding individual and group behaviour cooperatively in relation to culture, way of life, and work, and (3) facilitating development of positive social, developmental, and political values to encourage more cohesive communities. In short, religion can be a powerful, benign sociocultural force, encouraging motivation, inclusiveness, participation, and sustainability. On the other hand, religion can be instrumentalised by those seeking to acquire or retain power, and sometimes their ends seem best served by extremism and terrorism, as in the case of modern jihadi groups (Haynes, 2005b).

Neo-nationalism: causes and consequences

The political importance of the coalescing of secular and religious and/or cultural concerns is illustrated by the recent emergence and political clout of neo-nationalism in the USA, Europe, and many other regions and countries.

Neo-nationalists are characteristically vocal about and defensive of their religion and/or culture. Contemporary neo-nationalists are often opposed to liberal policies on gender equality and immigration. In the 2010s and 2020s, such 'right-wing' neo-nationalists won power, or achieved a significantly increased share of the vote, in numerous countries, including Australia, Brazil, India, the USA, and several European states, among them the Czech Republic, Denmark, France, Germany, Hungary, Italy, the Netherlands, Poland, Slovakia, and Sweden (Haynes, 2019a, 2020b).

Neo-nationalists want strictly controlled immigration to protect and advance the nation's indigenous culture or religion and advocate enhanced sovereignty to limit allegedly unwelcome foreign influences and people. For example, Hungary's neo-nationalist prime minister, Viktor Orbán, refers to 'the' people in a certain way, with a specific understanding of what the term means: he does not mean *all* his country's citizens, only native Christian Hungarians. Viktor Orbán privileges some citizens over others: Hungarians who are both practising Christians and politically conservative. Like Orbán, Trump is a neo-nationalist who is keen to represent and champion nativist – especially white – Americans,[2] rather than Muslim-Americans who he explicitly denigrated during both the 2016 presidential election campaign and his subsequent presidency (Haynes 2019b: 142–146). Marchetti refers to the linking of religion and culture with nationalism as 'civilizationism'. He explains,

> the civilizational model is centred on the primacy of the cultural and religious bond. . . . *Within the political and economic context of globalization, characterized by a high degree of political and economic exclusion, the perspective of civilizations offers grounds for a conservative rejection of global transformations.*
> (emphasis added; Marchetti, 2016, 122)

"Key factors contributing to conflict principally relate to the fact of irreducible cultural differences" (Marchetti, 2016: 123). Like Orbán, Trump proclaims 'irreducible cultural differences' between, on the one hand, Christians and secular people, and on the other, between nativist Americans and certain categories of immigrants. Neo-nationalism reflects a belief that 'desirable' religious and cultural concerns are fundamentally necessary attributes of a nation's citizens. It seeks to exclude or marginalise those who do not have such views or attributes.

Such characteristics animate neo-nationalists around the world, not only in the USA during the Trump presidency. In Russia, India, Myanmar, Australia, Canada, and numerous European countries, neo-nationalists regard Muslims as the Other, while Jews too are also vilified (Fox, 2020). This is because both Muslim and Jews are often perceived by neo-nationalists to have 'irreducible cultural differences' that cannot be resolved, whether by discussion, dialogue, persuasion, threat, or compromise. This is a highly political issue, of great importance during elections: can the neo-nationalist politician persuade sufficient voters not only that such differences exist but also that they are politically important enough to persuade voters to choose them and not their rivals? Buzan and Waever remind us,

> limited collectivities (states, nations, and as anticipated by [Samuel] Huntington, civilisations) engage in self-reinforcing rivalries with other limited collectivities and . . . such interaction strengthens their we-feeling. [Because this] involves a reference to a "we", it is a social construct operative in the interaction among people. A main criterion of this type of referent is that it forms an interpretative community: that it is the context in which principles of legitimacy and valuation circulate and within which the individual constructs an interpretation of events.
> (Buzan and Waever, 2009: 255)

In other words, vote for me and I'll save you from the bad guys. Who are the bad guys? Anyone sufficiently different from 'us' to warrant the term and which permits – or 'impels' – 'us' to be suspicious of 'them'. This kind of divisive rhetoric defines the political landscape for neo-nationalists.

Recent 'global transformations' encourage neo-nationalism. As Marchetti (2016) notes, the post–Cold War world has seen many often momentous political, social, economic, and technological alterations from the status quo ante. The changes were often manifested in a widespread and increasingly significant focus on identity, involving various religious and cultural – that is, 'civilisational' – configurations, which served to marginalise some citizens. In the early 1990s, political globalisation focused on an internationalist goal: how to bring about Western ideas of liberal democracy and improved human rights. It soon became evident, however, that the goal was a chimera. In recent times, the world has seen both widespread democratic backsliding and frequent and pervasive attacks on human rights. In many countries, neo-nationalists seek to benefit. According to Brubaker (2017), neo-nationalists seek to profit from "two sets of decades-spanning structural trends", involving four 'transformations': "party politics, social structure, media, and governance structures." Neo-nationalists promote "a generic populism – a heightened tendency to address 'the people' directly – and the demographic, economic, and cultural transformations that have encouraged more specific forms of protectionist populism". These changes interacted from the mid-2000s with a "conjunctural coming-together of a series of [security] crises": "the security crisis", consequential to a succession of terror attacks by Islamist extremists including and subsequent to 9/11; "the Great Recession and sovereign debt crisis" in 2008; and "the refugee crisis" of 2015, stemming from Syria's tragic civil war. These crises occurred "in the context of a crisis of public knowledge – to form a 'perfect storm' that was powerfully conducive to populist claims to protect the people against threats to their economic, cultural, and physical security" (Brubaker, 2017: 369). This is the backdrop for the political power of neo-nationalism today, reflected in frequent references to alleged cultural and religious differences to help fuel neo-nationalists' bid for votes.

Following the work of Theodore (2019), Hervik (2011), and Daigle, Neulen, and Hofeman (2019), Bergmann (2020) categorises the development of neo-nationalism in three waves. Bergmann's (2020) three 'waves' of upheaval were key factors in the political rise and global growth of neo-nationalism. The first wave occurred in the aftermath of the global oil crisis of 1972, when around the world oil prices rose unprecedentedly, which posed major and unexpected strains on the economies of Western industrialised countries. The second wave came two decades later, following the swift and unexpected demise of the Soviet Union as a result of the twin onslaughts of globalisation and demands for democracy and improved human rights. The third wave came in the wake of the global financial crisis of 2008 and was bolstered in Europe as a consequence of the 2015 refugee crisis. Following the research scheme – but not the periodisation – of von Beyme (1988) and Mudde (2016), Bergmann explores the main features of each of the three waves and the main differences between them. One interesting contribution of Bergmann's book is his connection of populism with nationalism in the rise of neo-nationalism in various countries, including the USA. For Bergmann, the political appeal of neo-nationalism is framed within countries' changing environments, related to topics such as liberalism, the economy, migration, and religion and culture.

Neo-nationalism in the USA

Neo-nationalism is an ideology articulated by political parties often described as radical, populist, or nativist (Svitych, 2018). A radical seeks to transform politics, seeking fundamental changes. A populist appeals to 'the people', pitting them against 'the elites'. A nativist wants to protect the interests of native-born or established inhabitants against those of immigrants. Trump portrays himself as a radical, someone who wants to turn on its head politics in the USA. Trump is also a populist, seeking to appeal to the mass of ordinary citizens, inviting them to condemn the self-serving elites, especially those who run the country. Finally, Trump is a nativist whose main body of supporters are white indigenous Americans. Taken together, the three attributes – radical, populist, nationalist – coalesce in neo-nationalism in the USA.

Neo-nationalists have recently enjoyed electoral success not only in the USA but also in many countries in Europe and elsewhere, such as Brazil and India. Strategies and electoral platforms are not identical. What occurs in individual countries is affected by "nationally specific factors such as political history, system and culture" (Greven, 2016). Having said that, neo-nationalists do have generic ideological similarities, which tends to inform their political messages, platforms, and programmes. First, neo-nationalists are also very often populists, pointing to a (supposedly corrupt) elite political class, from which the mass of the ordinary people needs defending. The populist neo-nationalist depicts him- or herself as a 'genuine' popular voice in opposition to the corrupt power holders. Second, neo-nationalists claim to champion the rights and legitimacy of the indigenous 'ordinary people' against the 'immigrant-loving' self-serving politics and business elites. The latter is said to want mass immigration for their own economic reasons: to flood the jobs market with myriads of 'foreigners' willing and able to work for relatively low wages and thus undercut the wage levels that native workers expect. According to Huntington (2004: 268), "these transnationals have little need for national loyalty, view national boundaries as obstacles that thankfully are vanishing, and see national governments as residues from the past whose only function now is to facilitate the elite's global operations". Third, as already noted, neo-nationalists typically vilify Islam as a faith and Muslims as a community, in ways reminiscent of the lack of support for Jewish refugees in the late 1930s and early 1940s in the USA and many European countries (Friedman, 1973; García, 2018).

Populism is often described as a 'thin' ideology that "considers society to be ultimately separated into two homogeneous and antagonistic camps, 'the pure people' versus 'the corrupt elite'" (Mudde, 2007: 23). Ekström, Patrona and Thornborrow (2018: 2) note that populism can be either 'left-wing' or 'right-wing'. The term right-wing, however, is analytically difficult when thinking about neo-nationalism. Some modern nationalists are left-wing; for example, Syriza in Greece and Spain's Podemos, as well as individual politicians, such as Bernie Sanders in the USA. In addition, some right-wing neo-nationalists prefer a social democratic-style welfare state compared to one where 'market forces' take precedence; in conventional political science terminology, this would not make them right-wing. Consequently, the designation of right-wing is analytically problematic when referring to neo-nationalism. This is because many parties so described prefer a social democratic-style welfare state rather than one where market forces take precedence. Where the designation right-wing comes in is when neo-nationalists claim that their country is primarily meant for those who 'belong', that is, people who qualify because of their ethnicity, not necessarily because they have citizenship. Trump's neo-nationalism combines adherence both to market forces and to nativism. Another key characteristic of his neo-nationalism is that both Trump and supportive media voices proclaim the cultural, political, and societal dangers of 'uncontrolled' Muslim immigration (Haynes, 2020b).

What is the relationship between neo-nationalism and populism in Trump's rhetoric? Most Christian nationalists in the USA are strongly supportive of Trump, because they believe that he will advance their twin goals: re-Christianising America and advancing international religious freedom, especially for Christians in countries where they are persecuted. This draws on the belief that the United States was founded as a Christian nation, and for the country to thrive it is necessary to return to Christian values in personal and public life (Whitehead and Perry, 2019). While Christian ideals and symbols have long played an important role in American public life, Christian nationalism is an ideology which goes much further than, for example, asserting that the phrase 'one nation under God' belongs in the pledge of allegiance. Stewart (2020) argues that Christian nationalism is a powerful ideological component of the politically potent Christian Right, which first came to prominence during the Reagan presidency. The Christian Right is not however a political party or movement. It is a network of well-funded, ideologically motivated think tanks, advocacy groups, and pastoral organisations, with both American and international connections. Stewart (2020) claims that Christian nationalists seeks to acquire power so as to impose their religious vision on all of American society, and Trump is said to be the means to achieve that goal.

Bergmann (2020) explains that neo-nationalism, which draws on both religious/cultural and secular self-interest concerns, characterises numerous politically important politicians and parties in Europe, the USA, and elsewhere. He follows Kitschelt (1997: 46), who argued that in Western Europe in the 1990s two factors were the basis of right-wing parties' political platforms: "neo-liberal politics with authoritarianism and a policy of anti-immigration". Bergmann (2020) suggests that in the early 2020s, Kitschelt's 'winning formula' needs updating. This is because nativist populists' political successes are also linked to how they are able to associate a powerful message of pending external threat with an assertive style of communication, claiming to be the mouthpiece of the ordinary man and woman, defending them against the corrupt elites. Trump's neo-nationalism combines characteristics highlighted by both Kitschelt and Bergmann: aggressive style communication, neo-liberal politics, authoritarianism, anti-immigration, and external threat. To this we can add a further dimension:

fear of the undermining of what are believed to be the appropriate religious-cultural characteristics of a country.

To summarise: neo-nationalism in America today brings together both religious and secular concerns which were successfully tapped into by President Trump for electoral success in 2016. Christian nationalism is an ideology infused with religious understandings. America First nationalism, on the other hand, is primarily informed by secular concerns. Both Christian nationalism and America First nationalism coalesce in seeking to improve the position of America and Americans, both at home and abroad, in order to reinforce US national interest. Although Trump's neo-nationalism is contoured by the USA's unique history, culture, politics, and society, it is not a singular phenomenon, only present in the USA. Trump is not alone in finding political success with a nativist populist appeal expressed as neo-nationalism.

Globalisation and neo-nationalism

What does neo-nationalism represent in terms of political developments in the USA? The third wave of neo-nationalism began in the wake of the 2008 global economic crisis, occurring at the cusp of George W. Bush's and Barack Obama's presidencies and, by 2016, represented by Donald Trump's election as president. This wave of neo-nationalism had a major political impact. Many have commented that in recent years not only the USA but also many other erstwhile liberal democratic countries are turning away from longstanding 'liberal' foundations, becoming more authoritarian, populist, and neo-nationalist. Taken together, the three waves of neo-nationalism over the last half century mark a decisive turning away from liberal democracy and towards autocratisation, characterised by the widespread deterioration of democratic norms and values on both sides of the Atlantic (Luhrmann and Lindberg, 2019). Previously discredited and marginalised political ideas and their party-political vehicles have become normalised. In other words, political ideologies which were for long periods regarded as unthinkable have become mainstream, forming the basis of neo-nationalist electoral appeals, informed by nativist populist ideologies.

Both Kitschelt (1997) and Bergmann (2020) refer to 'anti-immigration' and 'external threat' as key terms in the lexicon of today's neo-nationalists. To the latter, growing immigration and threats to sovereignty are consequential to globalisation: it delivers 'too many' immigrants (including refugees, asylum seekers, and economic migrants), and many states seem powerless to stop them (Shai, 2020). Many would agree that globalisation is a process whereby the world is increasingly characterised by common activities, emphasising that many highly important aspects of life – including politics, culture, economics, trade, wars, and crime – are highly interrelated across national boundaries. In addition, globalisation is also a matter of ideational change, with people from various spheres, including politics, religion, culture, business, sport, and many other activities, thinking and acting in the context of a world which *de facto* is becoming 'globalised'. A consequence is that 'territoriality' – that is, the close connection or limitation with reference to a particular geographic area or country – now has declining significance. This suggests that globalisation implies greatly increased interdependence, involving both states and non-states: what happens in one part of the world necessarily affects (many) others, directly or indirectly. Globalisation also encompasses the idea that humankind is currently experiencing a "historically unique *increase of scale* to a global interdependency among people and nations". It has three main components: (1) continuing integration of the world economy, (2) innovations and international expansion of electronic communications, and (3) substantial increase in environmental, "political and cultural awareness of the global interdependency of humanity" (Warburg, 2001: 1).

Globalisation has deep historical roots. It is often said to have begun in the 1500s, encompassing three interrelated political, economic, and technological processes (Clark, 1997). Although globalisation is a continuous, historically based, multifaceted process, there have been periods when it has been especially speedy. For example, its pace increased from around 1870 until the start of World War I in 1914. This was partly because during those four decades, "all parts of the world began to feel the impact of the international economy, and for the first time in history it was possible to have instant long-distance communication (telegraph, radio) between people" (Warburg, 2001: 2). After World War II, the speed, density, and international impact of globalisation expanded again – as it did once more after the Cold War came to an end in 1989 (Haynes, 2007: 65–95). According to Keohane, the overall impact of these processes of globalisation resulted in an end-state: 'globalism'. For Keohane, globalism is

> a state of the world involving networks of interdependence at multicontinental distances, linked through flows of capital and goods, information and ideas, people and force, as well as environmentally and biologically relevant substances.
>
> (Keohane, 2002: 31)

Keohane explains that *globalism* refers to the reality of being interconnected, and refers "all the inter-connections of the modern world" and highlights "patterns that underlie (and explain) them" (Keohane, 2002: 2). *Globalisation* denotes the speed at which such connections flourish.

Globalisation is a continuous, multi-dimensional process with historical roots, with intensification of global interconnectedness involving both states and non-state actors. Finally, globalisation indicates a significant reduction in the importance of territorial boundaries and highlights major increases in multifaceted interactions. For neo-nationalists, it is politically expedient to blame globalisation for governmental failures. It creates a handy enemy and helps to rally voters in pursuit of neo-nationalist and against internationalist goals.

Globalists and anti-globalists

While there is much agreement about the analytical significance of globalisation, including its political and economic strands, there is little agreement about what it will lead to. Debate about its impact are polarised, rather simplistically: is globalism 'good' or 'bad'? One group – let's call them 'globalists' – expresses a generally positive perception of globalism. This view, associated with various politicians, including Germany's Angela Merkel and Emmanuel Macron of France, regard globalisation as potentially leading to a better world with more choice for consumers and the spread of human rights and democracy. This is a world characterised by strong popular support for enhanced international cooperation in order to progress a range of peace and development goals, a regime led by international organisations, especially the United Nations and regional bodies, including the European Union. The purpose is to address effectively multifaceted – economic, developmental, social, political, environmental, gender, and human rights – concerns and injustices. In short, globalists understand that the world has multiple problems and believe that the best way to address them is through international and transnational cooperation, with significant and continuous involvement by numerous sub-national entities and grassroots organisations, collectively comprising a powerful transnational civil society.

'Anti-globalists', such as Donald Trump, see the world very differently (Borger, 2019). For them, globalisation triggers a host of unfortunate and unwelcome outcomes, including restructuring of global trade, production, and finance to disadvantage some countries and provide advantages for others; growing numbers of economic migrants and refugees, who take advantage of growing ease and reduced cost of international travel to move, sometimes illegally, from poor to rich countries; and increasing international terrorism, with terrorists taking advantage of the internet and ease of travel to spread their murderous ideologies. Anti-globalism appeals to many neo-nationalist politicians. It facilitates attempts to exploit popular fears of an 'influx' of foreigners – as a perceived result of economic globalisation – for their own political purposes. While anti-globalist neo-nationalists might be prepared to admit that global free trade theoretically has a good side – including lower taxes and cheaper goods – for them this does not outweigh a less desirable outcome. This is a free(r) labour market and associated immigration, the consequence, they claim, of massive, 'uncontrolled' population movements from the poor world – for example, from Africa, the Middle East, and Central and Latin America – to rich Western countries. (Whether such a movement of labour is objectively beneficial for Western economies is rarely discussed by neo-nationalists.) In addition, today's neo-nationalists cultivate powerful media allies whose coverage of immigration is often that such population transfers frequently result in often serious "conflicts between immigrant and established communities in formerly tight-knit neighbourhoods" (Mittelman, 1994: 429; Haynes, Hough, Malik and Pettiford, 2017). Finally, these concerns frequently inform xenophobic populist propaganda which surfaces during national elections in many countries.

Conclusion

In September 2019, Donald Trump used an address to the United Nations General Assembly to "deliver a nationalist manifesto, denouncing 'globalism' and illegal immigration and promoting patriotism as a cure for the world's ills" (Borger, 2019). Trump claimed that leaders who were astute constantly

> put the good of their own people and their own country first. The future does not belong to globalists, the future belongs to patriots. . . . If you want freedom, take pride in your country. If you want democracy, hold on to your sovereignty. If you want peace, love your nation.

Trump also used the address to criticise "the system of global trade" and claimed that the World Trade Organisation "needs drastic change". In particular, he criticised China for "gam[ing] the system at others' expense" by employing unfair trade practices (Lynch, 2019).

At home, Trump's anti-globalism was expressed in his neo-nationalist policies, including attempts to strictly control immigration from Central and Latin America and bar Muslims from a number of countries from entering the United States via the so-called Muslim ban. The Trump administration's anti-globalist approach is also expressed in the regime's foreign policy, an issue we focus on in Chapter 4. Trump and his key foreign policy official, Secretary of State Mike Pompeo, believe that the United States is peerless, a special nation chosen by God to lead the world. This belief in the United States' global role is not new. For several decades following the end of the Cold War, the United States played a pivotal international role in 'democracy promotion', aiming to globalise the USA's democratic values, cultures, and institutions and expand human rights around the world. From the early 1990s until the late 2010s, the presidencies of George H. W. Bush, Bill Clinton, George W. Bush, and Barack Obama shared an aim: to advance and spread America's core 'civilisational' values – including representative democracy; religious freedom, especially the rights of Christians; and more generally, human rights. Both representative democracy and improved human rights were thought to be desirable in themselves. In addition, successive presidents believed that countries with such values and systems and were more likely to act in ways conducive to good relations with the USA and by extension the West more generally. Until the Trump presidency, successive US administrations had pursued international democracy promotion with at best limited success: while some countries democratised and human rights improved, others did not; it was very difficult to be sure that the influence of the USA was important in this respect. After a decade of promoting liberal democracy and improved human rights in the Middle East, sub-Saharan Africa, and the former Soviet bloc, US foreign policy was turned on its head by the al-Qaeda attacks on 11 September 2001. While the US did not officially jettison its pro-liberal democracy and human rights preferences, they were largely replaced by a different goal: elimination of the political ideology of radical Islamism, especially its violent extremist and terrorist expressions, unsurprisingly seen after 9/11 as a key threat to America's well-being and security. As a result of two key imperatives – democracy promotion and a post-9/11 security focus – the USA began to focus on national rather than international goals, a shift supported by both Christian conservatives and secular nationalists. During the Trump presidency, democracy promotion declined and a single human right – religious freedom – emerged as the administration's strong preference, enthusiastically and publicly endorsed by both Pompeo and Vice President Mike Pence (Haynes, 2020a).

These concerns form the backdrop and subject matter of this book. Its purpose is to analyse the role of neo-nationalism both at home and in the USA's international relations in the presidency of Donald Trump. The aim is to provide an accessible, succinct, and persuasive overview of President Trump's exploitation of neo-nationalism to win the 2016 presidential elections and to explain the policies which followed. I argue that Trump's neo-nationalism draws heavily on nativist populism to the extent that it is difficult to imagine or characterise the former without the latter. In support of the argument, I shall show that one of the outcomes of Trump's use of neo-nationalism is to undermine the rights of millions of Americans, collectively identified as 'outsiders', 'foreigners', or 'terrorists'.

Notes

1 "Ideology is a set of principles or ideals that (typically) serve as the foundation for political, religious, or economic systems. Dogma is a set of rules established by an authority as true, regardless of evidence or outcomes." (www.quora.com/When-does-ideology-become-a-dogma)
2 "Nativism is the political policy of promoting the interests of native inhabitants against those of immigrants, including supporting immigration-restriction measures" (Wikipedia).

2 Culture wars and neo-nationalism

Chapter 2 examines the USA's culture wars over time. It explains that issues that inform the culture wars are also central to the neo-nationalism which came to the fore during the Trump presidency. For decades, the USA has been embroiled in divisive ideological conflicts pitting conservatives against liberals, which are central to America's current political and social polarisation (Chapman and Ciment, 2013). Gaston (2019: 231) explains that the USA's culture wars are "pitched battles over cultural and social issues such as abortion and gay marriage" (Lewis, 2017), focusing on "moral guidelines for personal behavior as well as . . . broader political norms – among them, freedom, equality, rights and dignity".

The culture wars of the 2020s had their roots in the 1980s. At that time, the Christian Right sought to make common cause on several domestic policy issues with secular neo-conservatives. The focus was on their 'freedom' allegedly being suppressed due to the influence of secularists, liberals, and progressives. Later, after 9/11, many among the Christian Right became Christian nationalists, lionising America and its 'Christian roots', contrasting the USA with al-Qaeda and its attack on 9/11 which killed around 3,000 people. This "apocalyptic contest between good and evil" (Halper and Clarke, 2004) stimulated Christian nationalism. After 9/11, many claimed that Muslims were inherently dangerous and, for the USA to be secure, both Islamist terrorism and Islam as belief system and set of values had to be both controlled and suppressed.

Beyond public perceptions and, more widely, views about immigration, America's culture wars reflect "deep disagreements on public-ethical matters like abortion and gay rights" which encourage "some groups to question the legitimacy of the political system as a whole" (Hefner, 2010: 93). James Davison Hunter was the first to examine systematically the culture wars in *Culture Wars: The Struggle to Define America* (1991). Hunter provides an influential account of how in the 1980s, Christian fundamentalists, Orthodox Jews, and conservative Catholics combined against liberals and progressives, jostling for control of American secular culture. 'Progressives' included religious liberals, as well as many Jews and secular Americans. The conflict was an escalating struggle to define American public life, increasingly polarised between two 'cultures'. Hunter (1991) regards the contrasting 'progressive' and 'orthodox' views as alternative systems of moral understanding. 'Orthodoxy' in this context includes viewpoints which hold that moral truth is static, universal, and sanctioned through divine powers. Progressivism, on the other hand, regards moral truth as both evolving and contextual. Over time, the two groups have been locked in a seemingly interminable struggle to assert control over various institutional and systemic entities in America, including those of the state, informed by contemporary cultural praxis.

It used to be said that American and foreign journalists rediscovered religion only every four years during cyclical US presidential elections. This is a reference to once periodic occasions when the media were alerted to the electoral possibilities of the Christian Right's votes. By the 1990s, this was a numerically large and politically influential corpus of millions of socially and politically conservative, mainly white Protestant evangelical, Christians. Despite ideological and political differences among its different entities, adherents of the Christian Right believe that secularisation leads inexorably to secularism, a state of affairs they regard as an existential threat, believing it aggressively excludes religion from the public realm (Green, Rozell, and Wilcox, 2003). The Christian Right wants to change this direction of travel, collectively promoting social and political goals to 're-Christianise' America. Key organisations within the Christian Right, such as Focus on the Family, the Family Research Council, and Wallbuilders, believe that the Christian Bible provides appropriate doctrines to live by; they are God-ordained and therefore not amenable to change or challenge from mere mortals. It is estimated that those claiming identification with the ideas of the Christian Right in the USA comprised around 20% (some 60 million people) of the adult population of more than 300 million (Green, Smidt, Guth and Kellstedt, 2005; Bates, 2006). Around a quarter of adult Americans adhere to an evangelical Christian denomination (Pew Research Center, 2014). This means that Evangelicals, most of whom are politically conservative, are the most common religious group just ahead of those without a religious affiliation. More than 60% (64%) of Evangelicals report church attendance at least weekly compared to around a third (35%) of other Christians, "suggesting a potential for a higher frequency of politically relevant messaging" (Husser, 2020).

While most white Christian conservatives, both Protestant and Catholic, voted for Trump in 2016, leaders of an important body of conservative Protestant Evangelicals do not support him. America's largest evangelical

38 Culture wars and neo-nationalism

organisation, the National Association of Evangelicals (NAE), "represents more than 45,000 local churches from 40 different denominations and serves a constituency of millions" (www.nae.net/about-nae/). In addition to its church membership, the NAE runs dozens of schools and non-profits, both in the USA and around the world, and "provides resources for ministry leaders and advocates for issues of 'justice and righteousness'". Thus, while

> many Americans view evangelicals through a political lens thanks to the media's focus on the strong white conservative evangelical support for President Donald Trump, NAE has been at the forefront of pointing out that *'evangelical' is a theological term that encompasses a politically diverse group of people.*
> (emphasis added; S. Smith, 2019)

The NAE opposes Trump for his immigration enforcement policies and pillorisation of LGBTQ people (Alexander, 2019), as well as for his personal amorality. NAE opposition to Trump, however, is not total. Like other Christian conservatives, Protestants, Catholics, and Mormons, the NAE strongly supports one of Trump's key policies of centrality to the culture wars: greater restrictions on the availability of abortion in America. A magazine close to the NAE, *Christianity Today*, published an editorial by its outgoing editor, Mark Galli, in December 2019, which strongly criticised Trump for his lack of moral compass (see Galli, 2019).

The division within America's evangelical community is reflective of a wider issue which polarises America socially and politically: the culture wars. They are highly controversial. As Bob (2012) states:

> [e]ven its name sparks controversy: Is it over sexual equality and gay rights – or sexual license and special rights? ... Hostile networks have grappled over whether to condemn human rights violations against homosexuals, whether to accept gay rights, and, most basically, whether sexual orientation and gender identity are legitimate concepts in [American law].

In addition, America's culture wars have become internationalised and prominently played out at the United Nations (Bob, 2012: 38; Haynes, 2020a). Coinciding with the most recent 'wave' of neo-nationalism, moral issues such as abortion and gay rights are key aspects of a global struggle between the religiously 'orthodox' and religious and secular liberals (Lewis, 2017). We turn to this issue in Chapter 4.

In the next section, we survey the relationship between the culture wars and the Christian Right. The following section examines links between the culture wars and secularisation. The third section appraises the relationship between America's culture wars and the decline of civil religion. The fourth section examines the impact of neo-nationalism on societal polarisation in the USA. A concluding section summarises the arguments of the chapter and sets the scene for Chapter 3, which looks at the attempts of Christian nationalists to amend the politics and political culture of the USA.

The Christian Right and culture wars

Key terms used in this book, including Christian Right and Christian nationalism, are not fixed, but vary depending on the context and the inclinations of the analyst. For example, Sara Diamond's (2000) understanding of the Christian Right includes its electoral clout, focusing on the boundaries and intersections where politics and culture converge. In this context, she examines a network of grassroots cultural institutions, including publishing houses, law firms, broadcast stations, and church-centred community programmes that have helped Christian conservative groups to build their political influence over time. Diamond highlights the Christian Right's alliance with the Republican Party, identifying organising strategies of powerful national organisations such as Focus on the Family and the Christian Coalition. Finally, Diamond examines how the rubric of 'family values' is used by the Christian Right to infuse their beliefs into local and national discussions around various issues, including childrearing, gay rights, abortion, public education, and funding for the arts (Lewis, 2017).

Gagné (2019) defines the Christian Right as a religious coalition with political aims. It mainly comprises Protestant Evangelicals and conservative Catholics and mainline Protestants. Many are ethnically 'white', descended for the most part from north-west European Protestants who historically migrated to the USA. Trump's electoral support draws heavily on the Christian Right, in the main Republican voters for both ideological and cultural reasons (Miller, 2019). The Christian Right is not a party, movement, or organisation. It is a loose partnership of individuals and groups united in the view that America's Christian foundations are undermined by secularisation and it is crucial to reverse this trend to return to what the Christian Right believes are America's founding values. Lacking organisational unity, the Christian Right does not have a collective view of what tactics and strategy are necessary to achieve re-Christianisation of America. One thing the Christian Right collectively agrees on is that a Trump presidency was necessary in order to attain a re-Christianised America. In the November 2016 presidential election, Trump attracted the support of four in five white Protestant evangelical voters, a greater proportion than fellow Republicans Mitt Romney, John McCain, or George W. Bush had achieved in the previous three elections. In addition, Trump gained the votes of more than half (56%) of white Catholics, with Hillary Clinton receiving only 37% (Sullivan, 2019). The support of white conservative Christians was almost certainly not because of Trump's personal religiosity or his recognisably Christian characteristics: he is "a thrice-married adulterer with previously socially liberal views" (Haberman, 2018). It was because Trump, a self-proclaimed nationalist, promised both to re-Christianise America and to 'make America great again' via his policies. Both Christian and secular conservatives believed in his promises and many voted for him in 2016.

The term 'Christian Right' generally refers either to a broad community of generic Christian conservatives or to a smaller subset of institutionalised Christian organisations pursuing goals collectively characterised by cultural, social, and political conservatism. The Christian Right differs from Christian nationalism in that the latter wants to achieve a state characterised by institutions reflective of America's perceived traditional Christian values and beliefs. Trump's neo-nationalism drew on the concerns of the country's culture wars, reflecting the concerns of both Christian nationalists and America First nationalists, while seeking to rebuild national institutions, such as the Supreme Court, to reflect his concerns. This policy shift was reflective of the growth of extreme partisanship in the USA, resulting in the virtual disappearance of the political centre ground. Drawing on the dogma of neo-nationalism, which attracted white Christian and secular conservatives in common cause, the Trump presidency actively encouraged the culture wars. Mainly white Christian conservatives and secular right-wing nationalists were ranged against religious and secular liberals. For President Trump and his supporters, neo-nationalism divides the world neatly into two: us and them, globalists and anti-globalists, religious and secular. Neo-nationalism is an ideological interpretation of the place and role of the nation, developed consequentially to America's culture wars and the impact of globalisation.

Culture wars and secularisation

> Perhaps no aspect of the American founding is as politicized today as the role of religion. . . . [L]iberals . . . see religious pluralism and equality as definitive American values, while conservatives . . . insist that [America] was founded as a Christian nation and . . . fostering . . . Christian, or Judeo-Christian, identity is essential.
>
> (Haselby, 2017)

President Trump owed his election victory in 2016 to the combined support of white Christian nationalists, who ideologically dominate the Republican

Party, and white secular conservatives. In 2020, as the presidential election drew near, the Republican Party supplied both the president and the Senate majority, although not the Congress, which the Democrats captured in the November 2018 mid-term elections. Encouraged by senior members of the Trump administration, including the president, Vice President Pence, and Secretary of State Pompeo, Christian nationalists did all they could to win the culture wars, fearful that the next president might not be Donald Trump but his Democrat challenger, Joe Biden. Attempts to win the culture wars were undertaken mainly by legislative means at the state level and federally through Trump's appointment to the Supreme Court of conservative judges. In October 2020, following the death of the liberal Ruth Bader Ginsburg, a white Catholic conservative, Amy Coney Barrett, was appointed to the Supreme Court by President Trump. This provided the Court with a perceived 6–3 conservative majority, thought likely to have a pivotal impact on issues central to the culture wars, including abortion, school prayer, and gay rights.

It is clear that although the USA is secularising, religion is not relegated to the periphery of politics or society. What then does secularisation mean in this context? The answer depends largely on how one chooses to judge the hold that religious sensibilities retain in America. If the societal vigour of religion is measured by the breadth of commitment to religious institutions and leaders and the persistence of associated ritualised behaviour, then the US experience – judged by figures of religious adherence which indicate that the USA has approximately twice as many religious observers compared to Western Europe – falsifies modernisation theory, which regards modernisation as axiomatic with secularisation. On the other hand, when applied to the USA, many observers note the inadequacies of what may be a rather naïve or uninformed form of the secularisation hypothesis.

Thirty years ago, Wald (1991: 244–245) stated that many Americans had

> strong loyalties to their faiths and experience religion as a significant force in their lives. . . . Religious enthusiasm in the United States may ebb and flow but it has *not* followed the steady downward spiral predicted by the naive version of the modernization model.

A more sophisticated version of the secularisation hypothesis focuses on the *depth* and *quality* of commitment as a society's suitable index of religiosity. From this perspective, the impact and extent of modernisation and secularisation in America is apparent in the degree to which religion is "a private matter for individuals, compartmentalized in the form of conscience, rather than as a vital force in public arenas" (Wald, 1991: 243). Drawing on then recent poll data, Wald (1991: 245) concluded "that formalized religion commitment vastly overstates religious consciousness in the American mind".

Thirty years after Wald (1991) wrote, many Americans – between one-third and three-quarters – considered that religion was losing influence in their society (Pew Research Center, 2018). Despite this, in the USA religion continued to manifest institutional strength. This was reflected both in comparatively high numbers of self-proclaimed believers and regular attendance at religious services and in numerous religious entities regularly engaging in public debates, discussion, and lobbying. This questions the idea of a declining *public* role for religion, even when for many Americans religious faith is an increasingly *private* matter. A more individualistic religious perspective is now common among Americans, including the rapid growth of 'religious nones' who now comprise a quarter of adult Americans, making no religious belief the second largest group in the USA. In this sense, religion is rapidly declining, a result of changing values – informed by personal and group decisions. As religion loses its grip on the minds and thought processes of many Americans, especially among the young, it points to a cleavage between declining numbers of Americans who believe that the USA was and should remain a 'Christian nation' and those Americans who believe strongly in religious pluralism without a predominant role for traditional Christian beliefs. This does not represent a clear change in the form of linkage between religion and politics: it is not desacralisation of the mass political realm, which the secularisation thesis claimed would happen consequent to modernisation. Today's America is religiously contoured by both fragmentation and voluntarism, shaping how religion intersects with mass political and social life.

During the Trump presidency, the fight for religion's public political role is a key factor in America's culture wars. The key issue is: what *should* religious actors be allowed to contribute to political life in the USA, given the constitutional constraints? Some contend that the language of the First Amendment of the US constitution – that is, "Congress shall make no law respecting an establishment of religion or prohibiting the free exercise thereof" – significantly restricts religion's ability to engage in politics, de facto condemning them to separate realms and forever dividing them. Others argue that the First Amendment is primarily about protecting religion from the state, implying that it is entirely appropriate that religion has public religious views and roles. This argument – that is, over the allowable limits of "religious expression by public authority" (Wald, 1991: 238) – is the substance of the culture wars. As already noted, the controversy is not new: the US political system has long provided a fertile environment for the expression of religious differences in the public realm. What is different is that the controversy extends to encompass neo-nationalism in the USA.

This topic is the focus of Chapter 3, which examines the impact of neo-nationalism on domestic political outcomes, including those linked to the culture wars.

Constitutionally, the USA is a secular state, that is, the governmental apparatus is formally independent of religion. Nevertheless, religious issues are often of great important to politics. Although 65% of Americans state that they are Christian (Pew Research Center, 2019), churches do not enjoy a favoured constitutional role; the rights of citizenship are not reserved only for Christians; and secular, not religious law, formally regulates citizens' conduct. Yet, secularisation is not *only* about a formal divorce of Church and State; in secular societies, for example those in France, the United Kingdom, and Sweden, public attitudes to religion range from indifference to outspoken hostility (Kuenkler, Madeley, and Shankar, 2019). In the early 2020s, the USA was, like others in the West, said to be increasingly a secular society (Pew Research Center, 2019). Christian nationalists sought to reverse the trend via legislation, not by exhortations to Christian morality.

Today's Christian nationalists have their roots in variously named religiously informed conservative movements, such as Jerry Falwell's 'Moral Majority', the 'Religious Right', and the 'Christian Right' (Diamond, 2000). Christian nationalists claim to be defending 'Christian values' against the onslaught of secularisation, seeking to reverse secularisation and liberalism, including legal abortion, absence or downgrading of prayers in state-run schools, and science teaching that adopts a rationalist, rather than a 'creationist', perspective (Halper and Clark, 2004). Until the presidency of Donald Trump, its achievements were modest. The issues on which it focuses – that is, abortion, sexuality, and attempts to defend religion (as in the case of 'creation science') against the claims of science – are regarded by many Americans as matters of personal preference, not political diktat (Pew Research Center, 2019).

Many Christian nationalists look to the Moral Majority, founded by Jerry Falwell in 1979, as the starting point of their movement (Diamond, 2000). Falwell emphasised the interfaith character of the Moral Majority, employing the term Judeo-Christian, to describe its umbrella approach, explicitly linking Jews and Christians in a collective endeavour (Sarna, 1982). Over time, however, the presence of Jews in the Moral Majority declined, and it became overtly Christian (Gaston, 2019: 240–244). During the 1980s, the Moral Majority became overwhelmed by financial problems. Falwell disbanded the Moral Majority in 1989 in Las Vegas, announcing, "Our goal has been achieved. . . . The religious right is solidly in place and . . . religious conservatives in America are now in for the duration" (Allitt, 2003: 198). Following the demise of the Moral Majority, the designations Religious Right or Christian Right were typically used to describe the movement. White Protestant conservative Evangelicals and white Catholic conservatives comprised most of its support.

Several landmark Supreme Court decisions underlined the concerns of the Moral Majority and its subsequent manifestations in the Religious and Christian Right. For example, in 1962 and 1963, the Supreme Court removed prayer and mandatory Bible reading from public schools. In 1965, the Hart-Cellar Act increased America's diversity by opening the country to large numbers of non-Western immigrants, some of whom brought with them diverse religious beliefs, including Islam, Hinduism, and Buddhism. In 1971, the Supreme Court, in *Green v. Connolly*, stripped the tax-exempt status from institutions that discriminated in their admissions policies based on race. *Green v. Connolly* affected a host of mainly Southern Christian schools and academies, many of which perceived the decision in terms of 'big government' threatening religious freedom – that is, their liberty to discriminate based upon a particularistic reading of the Bible, while undermining the supposed Christian foundations of America. In 1973, the Supreme Court supported a women's right to an abortion in *Roe v. Wade* (Lewis, 2017). Many Christian conservatives regard *Roe v. Wade* as expressly going against God's will, believing that every child is a gift from God (DiMaggio, 2019: 159–172). The overall result was that over a decade – the early 1960s to the early 1970s – the world that white Christian conservatives had grown up in seemed to be fast disappearing. They did not like what they saw and wanted it reversed.

Prior to the 1970s, Christian conservatives were largely a subculture, keeping their distance from politics. But with a new focus on social conservatism, around the time of the presidency of Ronald Reagan (1981–1989), Republican Party strategists – together with neo-conservatives and other right-wing ideologues – encouraged the politicisation of conservative Protestant Evangelicals as part of the 'New Right' fusion that propelled Ronald Reagan to the presidency in 1981 and again in 1985 (Lewis Taylor, 2005). White Christian conservatives had begun by this time to organise politically. Buoyed by burgeoning interest in American identity, which came to a head in the USA's bicentennial celebrations in 1976, many came to believe that this was the only way to reverse what they perceived as the damaging effects of secularisation, encouraged by unwelcome social, cultural, and demographic changes (Fea, 2018: 58–60). Building on the desire to reverse secularisation by political means, Falwell's Moral Majority sought to "train, mobilize, and electrify the Religious Right" in preparation to fight a "holy war" for the moral soul of America. The support of Falwell and the Moral Majority played a major role in electing Ronald Reagan as president in 1980, helping shape the long-term goals of the Christian Right (Fea, 2018).

The Moral Majority gained political strength and popular support. Ronald Reagan saw the opportunity to gain votes from this constituency. Reagan was a highly influential voice of modern conservatism in the USA, a forerunner of President Trump in his ability to win the support of both white Christian and secular nationalists. Reagan encouraged religious conservatives to join him in focusing on America's social problems, which he claimed was a result of a calamitous moral decline in "Christian values", leading to unwelcome outcomes, such as increased availability of abortion and sexual equality, including for gays (McVeigh and Estep, 2019: 164). During Reagan's two-term presidency, the Christian Right became an increasingly powerful entity within the Republican Party. Its support was instrumental in George W. Bush's electoral victories in 2000 and 2004, although its political influence diminished during the Obama presidency (2009–2017). Trump's electoral victory heralded a return to political prominence (Bettiza, 2019: 218), reflective of the fact that the Christian Right now ideologically dominates the Republican Party. Its *raison d'être* has evolved from seeking a more Christian country to a vision of a re-Christianised nation characterised by (1) a strongly patriotic and nationalist culture and (2) political and social defeat of religious liberals, secularists, the LGBTQ community, and feminists. This is to be achieved by legislative means, not by exhortation to moral imperatives.

Culture wars and decline of civil religion

Culture wars developed and the once consensual idea of civil religion declined. What is the connection between the two developments? To explain what happened, it is useful to identify why religion retains clear political significance in the USA. Writing three decades ago, Wald (1991: 241) argued that religion was multifaceted, expressed

> through such diverse paths as the impact of sacred values on political perceptions, the growing interaction between complex religious organizations and State regulatory agencies, the role of congregational involvement in political mobilization and the functionality of Churches as a political resource for disadvantaged groups.

He explained that America's cultural, political, and social development were greatly affected by patterns of individual and group religious commitment, which encouraged religious differentiation. This led to a growing number of extant religions in the USA, often with divisions within them. It also resulted in religious voluntarism, that is, most people believe that religious choices are not necessarily an ascriptive trait, conferred by birth.

Instead, they are more a matter of choice and discretionary involvement. What is the situation today, compared to Wald's comments 30 years ago? Religious cleavages did not disappear as America modernised. Instead, they were redefined and extended to a growing number of social and political issues, expressed in the culture wars.

Following World War II, America went through a long period of rising prosperity and national optimism. At this time, America was said to be characterised by 'civil religion', a consensual non-partisan allegiance to a communal religious outlook. Society was believed not to be associated with any particular political or ideological position, reflective of a shared religious and cultural tradition, which had developed over time. The American state sought to cultivate 'civil religion' as the cult of the political community. Jean-Jacques Rousseau was the first to use the term 'civil religion' in his *The Social Contract*, published in 1762, while de Tocqueville (1969) examined it in the specific context of America. To Rousseau, civil religion was the American polity's shared religious dimension. Mainly through the work of Robert Bellah, civil religion became an important concept in the modern sociology of religion. He sought to define the concept as a demonstrative assertion of a shared civic faith, which had been of great social and political significance throughout the history of post-colonial America. In 'Civil Religion in America', an influential article published in 1967, Bellah identifies civil religion as the *generalised* religion of the "American way of life", existing with its own integrity alongside particularistic expressions of faith, including several Christian denominations and Judaism. Robbins and Anthony (1982: 10) understand civil religion as the "complex of shared religio-political meanings that articulate a sense of common national purpose and that rationalize the needs and purposes of the broader community". Thus, for both Bellah and Robbins and Anthony, civil religion advanced the idea that a post-colonial democratic United States was an agent of God, signifying that the American nation exhibited a collective faith serving a transcendent purpose. Political and religious spheres were constitutionally separate, and civil religion was regarded as the means to unite them, a crucial component of what it meant to be American.

Bellah saw civil religion as essential to restrain the self-interested elements of American liberalism, encouraging it toward a public-spirited citizenship which enabled republican institutions to thrive. Bellah saw civil religion as a fundamental prerequisite of a stable democracy, a necessary antidote to the United States' inherently pluralistic and individualistic culture. It was the glue that held society together, the key means by which Americans arrived at common societal values in a country built, on the one hand, on ideals of mutual tolerance and unity and, on the other, on great cultural and religious diversity. Civil religion made a highly positive contribution to societal integration, exhibiting a clear ability to bind a group of diverse people, who were nevertheless united in achieving a common goal, while imparting a sacred character to citizens' civic obligations and responsibilities.

The concept of civil religion also provided a means for public manifestation of religious faith, counteracting particular religious expressions' tendency towards individuality. However, just as Bellah was proclaiming the great importance of civil religion to the integrity of the United States, the country was being torn apart by societal strife which, in hindsight, can be seen as the opening shots in the culture wars. On the one hand, there was increasing structural differentiation of private from public sectors and, on the other, there were widening societal divisions: religious, racial, ethnic, and class. Collectively, these developments undermined the generalised acceptance of a shared conception of moral order. Bellah's mid-1970s' book, *The Broken Covenant* (1975), argued that social changes were destroying public confidence in US intuitions, fatally weakening consensual traditions that had historically sustained faith in the republic. The societal consensus, believed central to civil religion, was effectively shattered by national reverses and scandals, including the Vietnam War and the Watergate scandal. Adding to these specific social and political travails, American unity was further undermined by polarising disputes over racial, moral, and ethical issues. While the former mainly focused on the position of African-Americans and Hispanics, the latter included state prohibitions on gender- and race-based discrimination, abortion rights, increased rates of cohabitation, permissiveness towards sexual expression in art and literature, reduced sanctions against homosexuality, and a Supreme Court decision proscribing school prayer.

Taken together, these developments are indicative of a decisive shift from traditional Judeo-Christian morality to a new divisiveness in the late 1960s and early 1970s, where civil religion could no longer fulfil its traditional unifying role among Americans. It led to the Moral Majority, followed by the (New) Christian Right. As Wald (1991: 256) noted, "if the core of the concept" of civil religion is "the tendency to hold the nation accountable to divine standards, then the case can be made that US political culture has actually been revitalized by the rise of the 'New Christian Right' (NCR)". Rather than seeking to rebuild the consensus manifested in civil religion, the Moral Majority and the Christian Right mobilised against perceived unacceptable manifestations of liberalism, viewed as the engine of America's moral decay.

Culture wars and neo-nationalism

From the 1980s, religion was a focus of public struggles over an appropriate moral and ethical direction for America. More generally, the 1980s and 1990s were a time of societal upheaval and division in the USA, as the country was roiled by profound economic, political, and cultural insecurities. There were external shocks – including the unforeseen ending of the Cold War, the unexpected demise of the Soviet Union, and globalisation; all impacted significantly on the USA and its social, economic, and political equilibrium. An earlier book of the current author, published in 1998, sought to capture a picture of America in turmoil:

> Angry white people blame African-Americans and immigrants for taking their jobs. Unemployed African-Americans look to blame the Hispanics. Forty million Americans have no health insurance, while blue-collar wages have fallen by nearly 20 per cent in real terms since the 1970s. Middle management is regularly 'downsized', while manufacturing jobs relocate to low-wage countries in Asia and Latin America. Meanwhile, the richest 2 per cent of the population control the majority of the wealth (Abramsky 1996: 18). A single company, communications giant AT&T shed 40,000 jobs in the mid-1990s, while its chief executive enjoyed a $5 million (£3.2 million) rise in the value of his share options. In short, the USA is racked by scapegoating and chronic insecurity in the 1990s.
>
> (Haynes, 1998: 23–24)

The purpose of the quotation is to illustrate that what was once a class-based, left-right, vertical political division in America had become by the 1990s a horizontal societal and political split. It divided, on the one hand, elites and the educated, who on the whole were believed to benefit from globalisation and, on the other, the 'left-behinds'. These were less privileged Americans further down the socio-economic pyramid. They believed their own positions were declining and, understandably, wished to reverse things. Who to blame?

Some politicians were quick to exploit the prevailing conditions of uncertainty, instability, and growing insecurity for their electoral advantage. For example, in the 1990s the unsuccessful presidential bids of Pat Buchanan, a Republican, were built primarily on populist appeals to the socio-economic 'left-behinds' that he would reverse their declining position. Buchanan is a conservative Catholic and economic nationalist and was the White House communication director in 1985–1987 during Richard Nixon's presidency. In 1992, following a failed bid to become the Republican Party's presidential candidate, Buchanan made what is known as his 'culture war speech', when he derided liberals as the cause of America's turmoil, claiming, "The American people are not going to go back into the discredited liberalism of the 1960s and the failed liberalism of the 1970s" (Buchanan, 1992). In 1996, Buchanan achieved credible but surprising victories in several early Republican caucuses and primaries. In 2000, he ran again unsuccessfully for the presidency with the slogan 'America First!' (NPR, 2017). Some have claimed that Buchannan is the man who made President Trump possible by airing an earlier version of neo-nationalism, whose central tenets Trump adopted two decades later (Mann, 2019).

Buchanan claimed that, if elected president, he would withdraw America from both the North American Free Trade Association and the World Trade Organization. His stance was reminiscent of that of leaders of the mid-19th-century populist party, the Know-Nothings, which pitted itself against the economic power of the eastern establishment who looked to internationalism for their – and America's – future prosperity. Given the manifest economic insecurity affecting many millions of Americans in the 1990s, it was not surprising that Buchanan's brand of populist economic nationalism appealed to significant numbers of mainly blue-collar Americans. In particular, he attracted many of the so-called Reagan Democrats, that is, disaffected unskilled or semi-skilled industrial workers fearing for their jobs in the 1990s in the wake of a progressively globalising economy. Buchanan polled relatively well in areas of the country where white Christian conservatives are plentiful, including Missouri and Louisiana. However, as a conservative Catholic, Buchanan found his electoral potential reduced among such states' white conservative Protestant majority.

Buchanan is worthy of note when seeking to explain the political ascendancy of Donald Trump two decades later. Like Trump, Buchanan is a right-wing populist who shares an 'America First' economic nationalism and expresses disdain for America's internationalist aspiration and obligations. However, a key difference between Trump and Buchanan is that the former understands the importance of Christian conservative support as, allied with that of America First nationalists, it was just enough to propel him to the White House, especially as he was competing against a relatively unpopular Democratic presidential candidate, Hillary Clinton. Buchanan was unable to recruit the support of the Christian Right *en masse* in support of his presidential bids. At the time, Republicans preferred a less divisive presidential candidate in the incumbent president, George H. W. Bush (who nevertheless lost to Bill Clinton in 1992). Trump did not repeat Buchanan's mistake: he assiduously cultivated both the Christian Right and the secular right to win the 2016 presidential election.

The Trump administration pursues Christian nationalist-friendly policies for both transactional and ideological reasons. A transactional relationship is one whereby both parties believe they are gaining something from the arrangement. Christian nationalists voted for Trump for his appointment of conservative Supreme Court judges, his vocal support for further controls on abortion availability, encouragement of Christian prayers in schools, and his claim to want to enhance 'religious freedom'. Many Christian nationalists also voted for Trump for ideological reasons, that is, like secular conservatives, they favourably regard his 'America First' policies as "standing up for America by imposing draconian controls on illegal immigration and confronting foreign partners on their allegedly unfair trade practices" (Crary, 2019).

Many non-religious conservatives also support such policies, providing another segment of his support base. Piacenza (2019) reports that in mid-2019 non-religious conservative Republicans were keener than their religious counterparts to see Trump re-elected president in November 2020. Why? Many such people supported Trump for his administration's economic record and his 'strong' 'anti-immigration' stance, targeting both 'Mexicans' and Muslims. Some among this group are white nationalists or supremacists. They are said to include Stephen Miller, a senior adviser and speechwriter for Trump (Holpuch, 2019). During the 2016 presidential campaign and once he was installed as president, Trump made much political capital out of his outspoken comments about immigrants, refugees, and Muslims (Haynes, 2019b). Miller was the author of many of Trump's speeches on the topic of immigration, a popular topic among his supporters, both Christian and secular (Holpuch, 2019).

Conclusion

Two things characterise many white Christian conservative voters and non-religious conservatives: (1) a shared list of grievances and (2) the belief that Donald Trump is the only president who can satisfactorily address them. The trajectory and outcome of the 2016 presidential election campaign indicated that Trump is adept at reading the signs of both groups' discontent, and he was able successfully to exploit them to his electoral advantage (Bacevich, 2020).

Trump's promise to reassert America's (Christian) foundational values gained the strong approval of Christian nationalists, while his assurance that he would strongly "stand up" for America globally was music to the ears of America First nationalists. White Christian conservatives, once the 'silent majority', were by this time a demographic minority. A nonpartisan research organisation, the Public Religion Research Institute (PRRI), published a report in September 2017, entitled *America's Changing Identity*. The report, which drew on a huge sample of 101,000 Americans from all 50 states, demonstrated that white Christians are now a minority among the US population. In the mid-1970s, eight in ten Americans were so identified, and more than half (55%) were white Protestants. By the mid-1990s, white Christians were two-thirds of the population (Jones and Cox, 2017). In 2017, the proportion of white Christians in the USA was 46% of what it was four decades ago. Many white conservative Christians felt beleaguered and regarded Donald Trump as their saviour. To achieve this, it was necessary to deepen and extend the culture wars, and Trump promised policies that met the approval of both sets of conservatives, both religious and secular. Today, however, as already noted, white Christians are no longer in the majority in the USA. Furthermore, recent opinion polls indicate that Americans are becoming more liberal on issues such as same-sex marriage, although not on abortion (Lewis, 2017). These two developments – numerical decline of white Christians and growing liberalism of Americans on some social issues – make it implausible that a re-Christianisation of America would occur through a large-scale, voluntary re-adoption of Christian conservative values. How then to bring this about? The answer was to try to revive and embed Christian conservative values via legislation, in order to win the culture wars. This forms the focus of the next chapter.

3 Neo-nationalism and politics in the USA

The election of Donald Trump in November 2016 was both a consequence and a proximate cause of America's political polarisation, which had been developing since the 1980s. Over time, America's developing culture indicated that the political centre ground had significantly shrunk. In particular, the concept of civil religion could no longer unite Americans as it had done in the recent past. By 2016, the societal divisions were stark: a majority of both the Christian Right and secular conservatives voted for Trump in the presidential election (Smith, 2020). Both of these sections of Trump's support believed he was the person to 'make America great again', to put 'America First', by significantly curbing non-white immigration, improving the existential well-being of native white Americans, and reasserting America's foundational Christian values.

Chapter 2 explained that by 2016 new patterns of group affiliation had emerged in America. They focused on various moral and social issues, including children's education, same-sex relationships and marriage, and females' access to abortion facilities. On such issues, there was "a pronounced attitudinal gap between practising Christians and non-believers", revealing distinctive religious preferences which do not conform to the historical dimension previously defining religious conflict on public issues (Wald, 1991: 265–266). The Christian Right's refrain of the necessity of repentance to put America back on the path of 'proper' morality was a central component of many politicians' rhetoric in their search for votes. Trump was, however, the most successful of them. But not until the presidential election of 2016 was it clear that the political power of both Christian nationalism and American First nationalism extended both to traditional and new social media and was highly influential in persuading many Americans to make up their mind about social and political issues and vote accordingly.

This chapter examines the impact of neo-nationalist policies on domestic outcomes in America during the Trump presidency. The first section explains the emergence of America First nationalism in the context of an earlier manifestation of dissatisfaction with the status quo: the Tea Party movement. The second section focuses on Christian nationalist policies. The third and concluding section summarises the concerns of the chapter.

America First nationalism: "we will not be ripped off any more"

"From this day forward, a new vision will govern our land. From this day forward, it's going to be only America first, America first." Donald Trump spoke these words on 20 January 2017 in the course of his inaugural address to the American people. It was a clear articulation of his neo-nationalism, highlighting that he would prioritise what he saw as American interests to the detriment of everything else. At first glance, there is nothing especially controversial about such a claim. At second glance, an uncomfortable question emerges: what does Trump means by the term 'American'? To many observers and 'ordinary' Americans, Trump's 'America First' nationalism is demarcated by race and rooted in disparagement for foreigners. Some see it a manifestation of ethno-nationalism manifested in policies, including the Muslim ban, the border wall with Mexico, and family separation of detained illegal immigrants (Lowry, 2019).

America First nationalists are primarily concerned about American jobs, immigration, and the country's global position. They believe that America is exploited by illegal immigrants, secularists, and some external powers to do the country down. America First nationalists believe that to 'make America great again' it is necessary to secure the country's borders and privilege national self-interest over internationalist concerns so as to bring back 'American jobs' and to project American values globally. America First nationalists are also wary of globalisation, widely seen as an important cause of America's perceived decline. In Donald Trump, America First nationalists believe they have a champion in the mould of Ronald Reagan. Reagan, like Trump, demanded increased attention to 'American values', which he articulated in a highly conservative and divisive manner.

Make America great again

Trump's 2016 election campaign slogan – "Make America Great Again" – chimed with the principle of America First: privilege the national interest, fix things at home, and let the foreigners sort themselves out. The MAGA slogan united many of Trump's supporters in a shared desire to return to the halcyon days of a white-majority Christian America, a time when the USA dominated the world militarily, diplomatically, and economically. The vision was to 'return' to a time when the 'American dream' seemed widely realisable, with strong and sustained economic growth, rising prosperity, and widespread get-up-and-go dynamism. For Trump's supporters, MAGA was also a campaign against the allegedly corrupt administrative/bureaucratic system, the 'deep state' and 'the swamp', targets which the Tea Party movement popularised in the early 2010s (Bergmann, 2020: 138–139). For many Americans, MAGA invoked the return of an 'old-fashioned', socially conservative worldview and lifestyle, when women knew their place both in the workplace and at home; ethnic and racial minorities had a subservient social and economic position and did not try 'too hard' to improve them via 'affirmative action'; and the USA was safe from external attack as a result of its nuclear weapons. Finally, MAGA informed the Trump administration's numerous trade wars with China, the European Union, Canada, Mexico, and Turkey. President Trump justified this policy, asserting that "we will not be ripped off any more". The claim was that trading partners had cheated ('ripped off') the USA for years in unequal trading relationships, while the USA haemorrhaged well-paid and skilled jobs to lower-income countries to their benefit and to the detriment of Americans, who as a result unjustly lost their jobs. According to Donald Trump, successive administrations were run by incapable or malicious chief executives who entered into multilateral agreements counter to US national interests, limiting the country's ability for unilateral action and ruining the economy. According to van Engen, "Trump based his first campaign on the idea that America was falling behind the rest of the world. 'America First' portrayed the nation as a place of carnage needing a savior to set it straight" (van Engen, 2020).

The concept of America First provided an opportunity for many of Trump's supporters to register their disfavour of lawmakers in Washington who appeared to them to be more concerned with own and other special interests, including 'fat cat' corporations and foreign countries, to the detriment of American workers. We saw in Chapter 2 that such issues had been raised in the 1990s by Pat Buchanan during his unsuccessful presidential bids. Echoes of Buchanan's 'America First' arguments persisted over the subsequent decades. They rose to the surface again during Barack Obama's presidency (2009–2017), stimulating the emergence of the Tea Party, "a loose congeries of grassroots groups and national advocacy organizations that vehemently opposed the Obama administration and advocated for conservative policies" (Sides, Tesler, and Vavreck: 37). These included "small government and lowering of taxes" (Bergmann, 2020: 124). The Tea Party was both economically and socially conservative. Many of its members and followers emphasised Christian family values, wanted enhanced security, and opposed amnesty for illegal immigrants. In addition, many forcefully campaigned against women's rights to abortion. During the 2016 presidential election campaign, Trump "advocated the cohabitation of both Christianity and American nationalism. Quite smoothly he emerged as the heir to the heritage of Reagan, [Newt] Gingrich and the Tea Party" (Bergmann, 2020: 188). They all "promoted the aggressive protection of US interests around the world" (Bergmann, 2020: 125), encapsulated in the slogan: 'America First'.

America First nationalists believe that globalisation leads to America losing out to competitors and rivals. As Trump put it in January 2017, "America first" means "we will not be ripped off any more" (Calamur, 2017). For Trump and America First nationalists, undesirable consequences of globalisation include the restructuring of global trade, seen to disadvantage the USA; growing numbers of migrants and refugees illegally trying to enter the USA, especially from Central and Latin America; and increased incidence of international terrorism in the USA and elsewhere. During the 2016 presidential election campaign, Trump sought to exploit for political gain widespread fears among Americans of an 'influx' of illegal immigrants, refugees, and foreign terrorists. While America First nationalists might be prepared to admit that global free trade theoretically has a good side – potentially, lower taxes and cheaper goods – for them it did not outweigh the downside: increasing numbers of foreigners, including economic migrants, resulting in large population movements from Mexico and Central America to the USA, unwelcome political refugees and, potentially, terrorists. Potential benefits of some immigration as beneficial to the American economy are rarely accepted by America First nationalists. Notable among the ranks of American First nationalists are not only President Trump but also senior politicians, such as Senator Steve King (Iowa) and key members of his administration, including Stephen Miller, chief speechwriter, and Steve Bannon, former chief strategist (Haynes, 2017).

Immigration reform

America First nationalists believe that culturally, socially, and politically, US principles and achievements have their roots in the country's Judeo-Christian values. This view was politically weaponised in recent years. Some groups, including 'Mexicans' and Muslims, were consequently vilified. Steve King called immigrants "dogs" and "dirt" while, when a presidential candidate, Trump "infamously declared that most immigrants crossing the southern border were 'rapists and criminals' and pledged to ban all Muslims from entering the US" (Siddiqui, 2019). America First nationalists see illegal immigration as an unmitigated problem leading to increased crime and societal conflicts between immigrants and established communities in tightly knit neighbourhoods, formerly without significant numbers of 'outsiders'. Trump's first State of the Union address on 30 January 2018

> **Box 3.1 Immigration Reform That Will Make America Great Again**
>
> *The three core principles of Donald J. Trump's immigration plan*
>
> When politicians talk about "immigration reform" they mean: amnesty, cheap labor and open borders. The [American] Schumer-Rubio immigration bill was nothing more than a giveaway to the corporate patrons who run both parties.
>
> Real immigration reform puts the needs of working people first – not wealthy globetrotting donors. We are the only country in the world whose immigration system puts the needs of other nations ahead of our own. That must change. Here are the three core principles of real immigration reform:
>
> 1. **A nation without borders is not a nation.** There must be a wall across the southern border.
> 2. **A nation without laws is not a nation.** Laws passed in accordance with our Constitutional system of government must be enforced.
> 3. **A nation that does not serve its own citizens is not a nation.** Any immigration plan must improve jobs, wages and security for all Americans.
>
> https://assets.donaldjtrump.com/Immigration-Reform-Trump.pdf

restated America First themes related to immigration first raised during the presidential election campaign. The four pillars of his administration's programme for immigration reform were (1) a path to citizenship for DREAMers; (2) increased border security funding; (3) ending the diversity visa lottery; and (4) restrictions on family-based immigration.[1]

Immigration reform is a key component of America First nationalism, reflecting the fact that Donald Trump was elected US president when both anti-immigration and 'anti-Muslim' sentiment were 'hot topics'. The three core principles of Trump's immigration plan are shown in the Box 3.1.

To bolster his anti-immigration message, Trump employed 'clash of civilisations' rhetoric during his presidential campaign, a theme that continued after he became president, not least because it went down well with voters (author's interviews with #2, #4, #5, and #8). During the presidential campaign in March 2016, Trump stated, "I think Islam hates us" (Campbell, 2016). During his presidential tenure, he continued to express anti-Muslim sentiments. He made no clear distinction between 'moderate' and 'extremist' Muslims, or between the mass of 'ordinary' Muslims and the tiny number whom Trump refers to as "radical Islamic terrorists". Is this any more than simple racism? It is difficult to know where a 'feel-it-in-the-gut' racism ends and a more 'scholarly' 'clash of civilisations' outlook begins. Several knowledgeable interviewees identify Trump as both a 'racist' and a 'nativist' (interviews with #3, #5, and #7). A nativist is someone who believes that the rights of indigenous people are much greater than those of immigrants. For the Dutch political scientist Cas Mudde, nativism is

> xenophobic nationalism . . . an ideology that wants congruence of state and nation – the political and the cultural unit. It wants one state for every nation and one nation for every state. It perceives all non-natives . . . as threatening. But the non-native is not only people. It can also be ideas.
>
> (Mudde quoted in Freidman, 2017)

Education

President Trump refers positively to Judeo-Christian values, which are of central importance to the content and philosophy of children's education. Although what comprises Judeo-Christian values is contested (Gaston, 2019), they are generally regarded as epitomising traditional moral and ethical values and beliefs to which many conservative Americans, both religious and secular, adhere. Reflecting this, in September 2020, President Trump announced the establishment of 'The 1776 Commission'. The aim was to "promote patriotic education" and a "pro-American curriculum" in schools. Trump's announcement came during the controversial Black Lives Matter campaign, which during 2020 was a key political and societal issue in the USA. The purpose of the commission was to present an officially sanctioned counter-view opposed both to race theory and to *The New York Times Magazine*'s '1619 Project'. The latter examines the legacy of slavery in the United States. Trump claimed that such campaigns "teach our children that we were founded on the principle of oppression, not freedom". To teach critical race theory to children was, in his view, a form of "child abuse". The 1776 Commission would, according to him, advance a curriculum "that celebrates the truth about our nation's great history" ('The 1619 Project', 2020).

According to the president, the purpose of the 1776 Commission was to "tell the truth about our nation's great history". It was necessary, he asserted, because some American children were growing up without the 'correct' knowledge in this regard. Trump wanted to make it clear that in his view, the United States is "the most exceptional nation in the history of the world", whose foundations are Judeo-Christian values ('Executive Order on Establishing the President's Advisory 1776 Commission', 2020). Trump had constructed his 2016 presidential campaign on the basis that, because of the machinations of liberals and secularists at home and those of nefarious foreigners internationally, America was underperforming at home and in competition with other countries, especially China. The idea of the 1776 Commission was that America could only restore its fortunes and be great again by returning to foundational values (Wise, 2020).

Trump's claims echoed the rhetoric employed by President Ronald Reagan in the 1980s. In 1988, during the last political speech of his presidency, Reagan made the claim that an "informed patriotism" with "more attention to American history" would facilitate greater understanding of the noble foundations of the American nation. Like Trump 30 years later, Reagan pronounced himself concerned that some American parents did not teach their children "unambivalent appreciation of America". Also like Trump, Reagan blamed what he regarded as schools teaching modern, leftist indoctrination. Instead, he proclaimed, "We've got to teach history based not on what's in fashion but what's important". Reagan's two examples of the important in American history were the Pilgrim Fathers and Jimmy Doolittle, an American military general and aviation pioneer ('Transcript of Reagan's Farewell Speech to American People', 1989).

Like Reagan in his aim of 'patriotic' education, Donald Trump was orientating himself towards his Christian nationalist base which, as already noted, first came to political prominence during the Reagan presidency. Many Christian conservatives are very sceptical about the value of public school education. Moreover, polls show that such people are the least likely among religious groups to believe in systemic racism – which the 1776 Commission aims to debunk. In addition, many prominent Christian conservatives adhere to a history of the American nation that is not just great but also built on Christian values and beliefs (PRRI, 2020).

Such language was on display during President Trump's remarks establishing the 1776 Commission. For example, he referred to America's National Archives as "the sacred home of our national memory", while claiming he would do all in his power to defend "the immortal principles of our nation's founders". Calling for a curriculum to teach "the miracle of American history", Trump stated that America's youth should learn "to love

America with all of their heart and all of their soul", and pledged to "save this cherished inheritance for our children, for their children, and for every generation to come" (Wise, 2020).

This section has examined some of the promises made by Donald Trump during the 2016 presidential election campaign and his policies as president in relation to two of his key slogans: "America First" and "Make America Great Again". We saw that his electoral strategy was to link the decline of certain sections of US industry with the economic rise of foreign nations, notably China, while claiming that the latter unfairly exploited America, profiting economically and developmentally while the USA declined (author's interviews with #2, #3, #4, and #5). The second key component of Trump's electoral appeal, especially to America First nationalists, was his claim that he would dramatically curb illegal immigration from Mexico by building a "beautiful wall" which, he averred, Mexico would pay for. A third claim was that he would ban potential Islamic terrorists from entering the USA, because they posed an existential threat. More generally, Trump depicted "Islam" as a cultural and ideational challenge to the USA. Quelling its threat required policies both to limit the numbers of Muslims in the USA and to prevent the spread of *sharia* law (Haynes, 2017, 2019b).

President Trump spoke less about 'push' and 'pull' factors which are important in explaining why so many Mexicans choose to uproot themselves and their families to try to achieve a better life in the USA. While, objectively, the US economy greatly benefits from the willingness of hundreds of thousands of people to do menial jobs at low wages which many among the local Americans do not want to do, Donald Trump depicted the issue as an exceptionally important political 'hot potato' with many among America's voters open to the message that in order to 'make America great again', the country must strictly control illegal immigration from Mexico so to improve the life chances of native Americans. One of Trump's 'selling points' in the 2016 presidential campaign was that as president he would 'force' the Mexican government to pay for the costs of erecting a border-length wall between Mexico and the USA at an estimated cost of between $2 and $10 billion, as a "sure fire" way to control illegal Mexican immigration (Haynes, 2016). Finally, America First nationalism was also reflected in the president's campaign to reassert traditional Judeo-Christian values in education and in particular to present an alternative narrative to that presented by critical race theory. The aim with the 1776 Commission was to make the case that America's founding values were being forgotten during secularisation and the radical reordering of the American nation from one mainly comprising white citizens to one inhabited by a huge variety of people of various ethnicities, religions, and cultures.

Christian nationalism in America: remaking God's country?

> God and country are persistent themes in President Trump's rhetoric. In his inaugural address, he predicted Americans "will be protected by God." He told a crowd at Liberty University that the country is "a nation of true believers." He often links God and the military in a way that appeals especially with his evangelical supporters. "We are and will always be one people, one family, and one glorious nation under God," he announced in his most recent Fourth of July message. He tweeted that he and his fellow citizens would think of the men and women serving in the military and "thank GOD for blessing us with these incredible HEROES!"
>
> (Zubovich, 2018)

White Christians conservatives' votes have been a key issue in US presidential elections since the 1980s. Before Donald Trump, however, no presidential candidate was able to amass and retain so much support from this constituency. Why were many white Christian conservatives, especially Protestants, so keen on Donald Trump? What did he seem to offer – politically, culturally, religiously – which led them to vote for him? Sides, Tesler, and Vavreck (2019) argue that Trump's presidential victory reflected several factors, including many Americans' strong disaffection with the status quo – economically, socially, culturally, and politically – and a belief that America had taken a wrong turn. Some believed that this was due to the country's moving away from its foundational Christian values.

Katherine Stewart (2020) traces how the pro-Trump, Christian Right developed strength and political purpose during the Obama presidency. For the Christian Right, Obama had many 'faults': too liberal, supportive of gender and sexual equality, perhaps a Muslim, maybe not born in the USA. Stewart explains that from the end of the Cold War in the late 1980s until the Trump presidency nearly 30 years later, successive presidents did not consistently pursue policies which the Christian Right wholeheartedly supported. Trump's accession to power was dependent on his ability to enlist not only the fulsome support of the Christian Right but also that of less-religious conservative nationalists, including 'blue-collar' workers, especially men without a college degree (Sides, Tesler, and Vavreck, 2019). Christian nationalists wanted to see the USA both more 'Christian' and more 'nationalist'. Such people strongly supported Trump's policies which they believed help achieve these goals. They liked it when Trump promised to bar Muslims from a number of countries from entering the USA and cheered when he voiced doubts about the patriotism of Muslim-Americans (Haynes, 2017). Christian nationalists believed that internationally the USA had long been too liberal in its dealings with international organisations, such as the United Nations. They liked it when Trump said he would reduce America's internationalist commitments. In short, Christian nationalists supported Trump not necessarily because they believed he was an exemplary Christian but because for them he was the right man in the right place at the right time to do a difficult but necessary job: reassert the country's Christian values, on which they believe the nation was founded, in order to 'make America great again' and put 'America First'.

Religious freedom

The Christian Right's goal of defending 'family values' was portrayed as a component of a wider concern: protecting their 'religious freedom' in the face of what many regard as aggressive secularisation and growing secularism. Many assert, rightly, that religious freedom was a founding principle of the United States, a fundamental right of all Americans. This is stated in the First Amendment to the US Constitution (1791):

> Congress shall make no law respecting an establishment of religion, or prohibiting the free exercise thereof; or abridging the freedom of speech, or of the press; or the right of the people peaceably to assemble, and to petition the government for a redress of grievances.

Polarised views on religious freedom contribute to a growing sense of division in the country and help fuel the culture wars. The Pew Research Center reported in 2017, "[s]ince 1994, the average partisan gap has increased from 15 percentage points to 36 points", noting that today "the party divide is much wider" than it once was. Political division reflects the outcome of a long process whereby a once extensive political, social, and cultural centre ground diminished dramatically (Doherty, 2017). Division can be seen in religious terms, where the concept of civil religion – "referring to a power beyond government in public rituals" – could no longer unite Americans as a nation. Now, Hart (2017) claims, civil religion has been replaced by "uncivil" religion, involving "the normalization of demagoguery and relativism in the public square".

Thomas Farr (2001), head of the Office of International Religious Freedom at the Department of State during the presidency of Bill Clinton, avers that "religious freedom [is] one of the foundational human rights. To protect this freedom means protecting something common to every human being." However, despite Farr's claim regarding the "foundational" and universal nature of religious freedom, "religious freedom" is also a problematic issue in America as it appears that some religious groups receive (sometimes much) more freedom than others do (Fox, 2020). In short, religious freedom is a politically and ideologically laden concept, not an objectively simple or clear one, whose meaning can differ substantially from person to person and group to group.

For some, religious freedom is about individual preference, believing that people should not have to go against their core religious values and beliefs so as to conform to what the prevailing (secular) culture or government requires. The Christian Right understands religious freedom in relation to four key issues central to America's culture wars: (1) anti-abortion activism, (2) opposition to equal rights for LGBTQ people and sex education classes, (3) promotion of Christian prayer in schools and teaching of creationism and intelligent design, and (4) opposition to euthanasia. Some argue that these religious liberty concerns imply freedom for some, not all, while potentially encouraging prejudice against those with different lifestyles and values, including women seeking abortions, LGBTQ people pursuing equality, non-religious and secular people, and religious minorities, notably, since 9/11, American Muslims (Lewis, 2019; Forster, 2019; Beydoun, 2018).

Project Blitz/Free For All

According to Wessner (2003: 67), for decades the Christian Right has "politicked to take back the Supreme Court, the Congress, the public schools, textbook publishing houses, foreign affairs, and the Executive branch". The Christian Right is said to be well organised, financed, and focused (Stewart, 2020; Whitehead and Perry, 2020; Fea, 2018). Individuals with views attractive to the Christian Right, such as Vice President Pence and Secretary of State Pompeo, occupy senior positions in the Trump administration (Haynes, 2020b). With its significant political influence, the Christian Right has brought new energy to a key Christian nationalist goal: re-Christianisation of America. To achieve this goal, the Christian Right launched a flagship initiative, Project Blitz, in 2018.[2] Project Blitz is a strategy and programme to achieve Christian Right goals via legislative reform. However, because of adverse publicity, Project Blitz was renamed 'Freedom For All' in October 2019 (Clarkson, 2020).

Many Americans, especially the secular and religiously liberal, find project Blitz/Freedom For All highly problematic because of its goal of re-Christianising America via legislation. In 2018, 43 organisations, collectively entitled 'National Organizations United in Opposition to Project Blitz and Similar Legislative Efforts', created a coalition to publicise and oppose Project Blitz. The aim of Project Blitz/ Freedom For All is to advance the Christian Right's views on religious freedom via legislation at the state level, in effect to advance the Christian nationalist agenda of re-Christianising America via legislation, seen as more likely to succeed than persuasion as America secularises. The anti-Project Blitz/Freedom For All opposition claims that its successful outcome would undermine rather than enhance religious freedom for all Americans. It willingly accepts that religious freedom is of primary importance to the USA, protecting everyone – both those with religious beliefs and those without them. Project Blitz/Freedom For All is regarded as a concerted effort to undermine the balance in this regard with the power of the state used to try to

> impose the faith of some onto everyone else, including our public school students. *This effort seeks to transform religious freedom into a sword that can be used to harm others, undermining important civil rights protections and healthcare access, especially for women, LGBTQ people, those of minority faiths, and the nonreligious.*
> (emphasis added; National Organizations United in Opposition to Project Blitz and Similar Legislative Efforts, 2019)

According to Americans United for Separation of Church and State (Americans United, n/d), Project Blitz is a key element in a bigger trend towards Christian nationalist goals. The aim is to

> redefine religious liberty as a sword used to harm others instead of a shield that protects people. Its organizers' strategy is to pass an increasingly ambitious set of state laws, starting with bills that require prominently displaying "In God We Trust" and establishing Bible classes in public schools and escalating to laws that would permit religion to be used to justify discrimination.

These are Christian nationalist goals, designed to compel all Americans to conform to the values of America's Christian nationalists, regardless of whether they approve of them.

Project Blitz/Freedom For All's origins were in the Supreme Court's 2014 decision in *Burwell v. Hobby Lobby*. The Court ruled, "the contraceptive mandate promulgated under the Patient Protection and Affordable Care Act violated privately held, for-profit corporations' right to religious freedom" (Gerais, 2017). Encouraged by the Court's decision, several Christian conservative advocacy groups sought to develop a shared strategy to use First Amendment claims of religious freedom to fight against or establish exemptions to numerous public regulations and protections, including laws seeking to fight discrimination (Lewis, 2017: 8). Project Blitz created a package of 20 model bills, following the example of the American Legislative Exchange Council,[3] which had earlier sought successfully to exempt business owners and professionals from requirements that "they provide reproductive health benefits for employees or provide services to same-sex couples" (Wolfe, 2019).

Project Blitz/Freedom For All provides model legislation to state lawmakers seeking to implement policies which aim to protect and advance religious freedom in line with the Christian nationalist agenda (Shimron, 2018).[4] The main Christian nationalist organisations behind Project Blitz/Freedom For All are the Congressional Prayer Caucus Foundation,[5] the National Legal Foundation,[6] and Wallbuilders' Pro-Family Legislators Network. The strategy is to persuade sympathetic state legislators to pass laws both protecting and furthering Christian conservative ideas of religious freedom. To facilitate the goal, by 2020 dozens of states had established "state prayer caucuses". The latter serve as focal points for state-level legislation on key Christian nationalist issues: education, same-sex marriage, and abortion availability. State prayer caucuses are the state chapters of the national Congressional Prayer Caucus. The researcher Frederick Clarkson of Political Research Associates states, the "state legislative network now comprises some 950 legislators, organized into Prayer Caucuses in 38 states", with plans to organise 42 state prayer caucuses by the end of 2020 (Clarkson, quoted in Wolfe, 2019).

Despite its organisational advances and geographical spread, Project Blitz/Freedom For All found it hard going in the face of growing opposition, especially from secularists and religious liberals. Wolfe (2019) notes that following much adverse publicity from 2018, Project Blitz/Freedom For All

> had diminished success with its model legislation. According to a spreadsheet of Blitz-related proposed bills provided to Daily Kos by Blitz Watch, 38 out of 82 bills introduced nationwide have failed or been vetoed. Ten have been passed, and 34 are still in the legislative pipeline.

Opposition to the goals of Project Blitz/Freedom For All was linked to the belief that the project is informed by the ideology of Christian nationalism which involves imposing on all Americans the Christian nationalists' "Judeo-Christian values" (Gagné, 2019; Haynes, 2017, 2019a). Some Christian nationalists cleave to what is known as 'dominionist' theology. This is a group of Christian political ideologies that seeks to pursue America's national transformation via a government of Christians to rule according to their understandings of biblical law. The ultimate dominionist goal is Christian authority over society and politics to usher in "God's kingdom on earth". Dominionists believe that God is calling on them to achieve this, a view encouraged by their interpretation of a passage from the book of Genesis (1:26–28).[7] To establish God's kingdom on earth is seen as fulfilment of Jesus' prayer: "Thy kingdom come, thy will be done *in earth* as it is in heaven" (Matthew 6:10).

Dominionism is framed in terms of social and political transformation, whose parameters are contoured by what is known as the "Seven Mountains Mandate" (sometimes referred to as "the seven moulders or spheres of culture"). Desired changes would occur following transformation of seven "spheres" or "mountains": religion, education, economics, politics, arts and entertainment, media, and the family. Lance Wallnau, said to be "the most influential guru of the 7 Mountains Mandate", claim that to re-Christianise America does not imply that more people have to be converted to the faith. Instead it implies that people with the capacity to influence outcomes meaningfully are paramount. Only relatively few people are required in positions of power and authority to effect great changes across a range of areas, what he refers to as "the matrix".

> We are called to go into the entire matrix and invade every system with an influence that liberates that system's fullest potential. . . . *The battle in each sphere is over the ideas that dominate that sphere and between the individuals who have the most power to advance those ideas.*
> (emphases added; Wallnau quoted in Gagné, 2019)

Political analyst Fredrick Clarkson contends that those directing are "savvy purveyors of dominionism". Their strategy is to go slowly in order not to alarm people about their intentions. "But they live an immanent theocratic vision, and they sometimes cannot help themselves, such as when they describe the resolutions as seeking to 'define public policies of the state in favor of biblical values concerning marriage and sexuality'" (Clarkson quoted in Wolfe, 2019). A favoured way to seek to further and implement "biblical values" is by seeking religious exclusions from laws governing civil rights and professional licensing standards. The strategy, if successful, would assist in creating government by Christian nationalists in the USA (Rosenberg, 2018). Whitehead, Perry, and Baker (2018) describe the quest for "dominion" as the aim of Christian nationalists who consider that the Christian faith and their particular interpretation should be imposed on all Americans regardless of whether they agree with Christian nationalist goals. The best way to achieve this, given that persuasion seems not to be working, is to legislate in order to compel obedience to the tenets of Christian nationalism.

There are informal links between Project Blitz/Freedom For All and several senior members of the Trump administration, with goals of the former shared by some members of the latter. Christian nationalists include President Trump, Vice President Pence, Secretary of State Pompeo, and Attorney General William Barr (Fea, 2018; Muirhead and Rosenblum, 2019; Haynes, 2020b; Gaston, 2019: 266). D'Antonio and Eisner (2018) claim that senior members of the Trump administration agree with the Christian nationalist goal of dominionism, claimed by some commentators to be the ultimate objective of Project Blitz/Freedom For All; the current vice president, Mike Pence, is an advocate of dominionism. Wong (2019) claims that both Attorney General Barr and Secretary of State Pompeo also favour dominionist ideas. Mencimer (2020) asserts, "influential politicians like former Rep. Michele Bachmann (R-Minn.), a regular visitor to the Trump White House, former vice-presidential candidate Sarah Palin, and former Trump Energy Secretary Rick Perry fall into this camp", as does Secretary of Housing and Urban Development Ben Carson, according to Christerson and Flory (2017).

President Trump's Faith & Opportunity Initiative is a unit in the Office of Public Liaison tasked with outreach to religious groups. It is a potential source of interaction between the current administration and the advocates of Project Blitz/Freedom For All. The aim of the Faith & Opportunity Initiative is to coordinate activities of Christian advocacy groups at the federal level. "The initiative charged the Office of Faith-based and Community initiatives with informing the administration of any failures of the executive branch to comply with religious liberty protections under law" (Norman, 2018). Paula White-Cain, Trump's 'personal preacher' and key leading member of the President's Evangelical Advisory Board, was appointed head of the Faith & Opportunity Initiative in October 2019 (Ahmed, 2019).

Finally, there is the 25-person President's Evangelical Advisory Board, whose members regularly visit the White House. Its members include Michelle Bachmann, former congresswomen and member of the Congressional Prayer Caucus; Jerry Falwell Jr., president of Liberty University until his resignation in August 2020; Robert Jeffress, senior pastor, First Baptist Church of Dallas; Richard Land, president, Southern Evangelical Seminary; Johnnie Moore, author and president of the KAIROS Company; Ralph Reed, founder, Faith and Freedom Coalition; and Paula White-Cain, formerly senior pastor, New Destiny Christian Center, head of the Faith & Opportunity Initiative (Haynes, 2020a).

The President's Evangelical Advisory Board is an informal body with no official status. However, AU was sufficiently alarmed about it to write to the Committee Management Secretariat of the General Services Administration, which is responsible for overseeing federal advisory committees. The secretariat's response to the AU was to deny "that the Evangelical Advisory Board has been meeting as a formal advisory committee. Some of the evangelical leaders involved also publicly denied that they meet as a formal advisory committee". From that time, that is mid-2019, the AU stated that there were

> no new reports and no evidence that we've been able to uncover indicating that the evangelical leaders continue to function as a formal advisory board – leading us to believe that our letter may have had an effect on the extent to which they are functioning as a formal group.
> (Liz Hayes, 2019)

Protection and expansion of religious freedom centrally informs the goals of the Christian Right. This section has examined the Christian Nationalist pursuit of "religious freedom" during the Trump presidency, involving fighting against what the Christian Right sees as "aggressive" secularisation by attempts to encourage legislative changes at both state and federal levels. At the states level, Project Blitz/Freedom For All urges sympathetic legislators to enact laws dedicated to protecting or enhancing religious freedom as conceptualised by the Christian Right. There do not seem to be institutional links between Project Blitz/Freedom For All and Trump's White House, although there may well be informal ties between some members of the Trump administration and leading figures in the Christian Right, focused in both the Faith & Opportunity Initiative and the President's Evangelical Advisory Board.

Conclusion

America First nationalists are primarily concerned about American jobs, non-white immigration, and the USA's national interest. Many America First nationalists believe that America is being exploited by immigrants, secularists, and some foreign governments, such as that of China, to do it down and undermine the well-being of American workers. America First nationalists believe that to 'make America great again' it is necessary to seal the country's borders and focus exclusively on national self-interest rather than internationalist goals. America First nationalists are also very wary of the impact of globalisation, which is seen to be a root cause of America's recent decline. Finally, in Donald Trump, America First nationalists believe they found a champion in the mould of Ronald Reagan, president four decades earlier. Trump, like Reagan, called for a reorientation of America towards 'American values' and against an internationalist projection of American power.

During the 1990s, new patterns of group affiliation emerged in America. They focused on various moral and social issues, including the use of pornography, same-sex relationships and marriage, females' access to abortion facilities, and marital fidelity. On these issues, there developed "a pronounced attitudinal gap between practising Christians and non-believers", which revealed distinctive religious preferences which do not conform to the historical dimension previously defining religious conflict on public issues (Wald, 1991: 265–266). The – no longer, New – Christian Right's refrain of the necessity of repentance to put America back on to its path of morality became a central component of numerous politicians' rhetoric, a key component of their bid for votes. Not until the election of Donald Trump, however, was it apparent that the political power of Christian Nationalism, which over time extended to both traditional and new social media, was now in the driving seat. Christian Nationalists claimed to be the public voice of theologically conservative Christian Americans. Many regard the country's travails as punishment for alleged departure from traditional Judeo-Christian values and beliefs. For them, Trump was the leader to put America back on the path of morality and virtue.

Notes

1 "On September 5, 2017, President Trump ordered an end to the Deferred Action on Childhood Arrivals (DACA) program. This program shields some young undocumented immigrants – who often arrived at a very young age in circumstances beyond their control – from deportation. In 2012, President Obama issued the DACA executive order after the Development, Relief and Education for Alien Minors (DREAM) Act did not pass in Congress several times. The young people impacted by DACA and the DREAM Act are often referred to as 'Dreamers.'" (www.adl.org/education/resources/tools-and-strategies/table-talk/what-is-daca-and-who-are-the-dreamers)
2 Project Blitz timeline (to January 2020): www.au.org/tags/project-blitz
3 "The American Legislative Exchange Council is America's largest nonpartisan, voluntary membership organization of state legislators dedicated to the principles of limited government, free markets and federalism. Comprised of nearly one-quarter of the country's state legislators and stakeholders from across the policy spectrum, ALEC members represent more than 60 million Americans and provide jobs to more than 30 million people in the United States." www.alec.org/
4 The Project Blitz strategy is outlined in a 148-page playbook, including model legislation covering various topics, including displaying "In God We Trust" in public buildings, allowing religion-based discrimination, and "Establishing Public Policy Favoring Reliance on and Maintenance of Birth Gender" (Congressional Prayer Caucus Foundation, 2018).
5 The Congressional Prayer Caucus was founded in 2005 by Randy Forbes, then a US Representative from Virginia's 4th District. It is "a bipartisan group of 105 federal lawmakers who meet to pray and foster spiritual guidance for our federal government" (www.familyfoundation.org/blog-posts/tag/Congressional+Prayer+Caucus).

6 "Our mission: To prayerfully create and implement innovative strategies that, through decisive action, will cause America's public policy and legal system to support and facilitate God's purpose for her, all while conducting ourselves at all times with the utmost integrity and in such a way as to glorify the Lord Jesus Christ" (https://nationallegalfoundation.org/about/).
7 Three verses are relevant: 26. Then God said, "Let us make mankind in our image, in our likeness, so that they may rule over the fish in the sea and the birds in the sky, over the livestock and all the wild animals, and over all the creatures that move along the ground." 27. So God created mankind in his own image, in the image of God he created them; male and female he created them. 28. God blessed them and said to them, "Be fruitful and increase in number; fill the earth and subdue it. Rule over the fish in the sea and the birds in the sky and over every living creature that moves on the ground."

4 Neo-nationalism and America's international relations

The aim of this chapter is to examine how the Trump presidency's neo-nationalism affected America's international relations. It argues that, in line with the president's neo-nationalism, which found favour with both America First nationalists and Christian nationalists, US international relations reflects concerns of the domestic culture wars, which we examined in Chapter 2. Two aspects of the culture wars were especially salient to America's international relations during the Trump presidency: first, replacement of long-term US support for the post–World War II liberal international order by policies which primarily reflected American national interest concerns according to Trump, including when these went against the preferences of the USA's main allies. This was apparent in the decline in America's support for the universalist post–World War international human rights regime, as expressed in the Universal Declaration of Human Rights (1948) and long championed by the United Nations. Second, America's national self-interest was expressed in a particularistic policy, championed especially by Christian nationalists, to privilege international religious freedom above other human rights, such as gender equality and the rights of sexual minorities. Overall, the chapter assesses how neo-nationalist policies affected the USA's international relations during the Trump presidency.

The first section of the chapter examines Trump's neo-nationalism in the context of the decline of the post–World War II liberal international order. The second section of the chapter surveys the Trump administration policies on human rights and international religious freedom. The third section concludes the chapter and summarises the impact of Trump's neo-nationalism on America's international relations.

Putting America first: neo-nationalism and the decline of the liberal international order

Until the Trump presidency, successive US administrations pursued international democracy promotion and religious freedom as key components of the country's foreign policy and international relations. As a result, some countries were encouraged to democratise and to improve their human rights, including religious freedom. After the Cold War, the USA spent a decade promoting liberal democracy and human rights around the world, notably in the Middle East, sub-Saharan Africa, and the former Soviet bloc (Haynes, Hough, Malik, and Pettiford, 2017). US foreign policy, however, was turned on its head by the al-Qaeda attacks on 11 September 2001. While the US did not officially jettison its liberal democracy and human rights preferences, they were partially overshadowed and replaced by a new goal: elimination of Islamist violent extremist and terrorism.

Liberal democracy and universal human rights are characteristic of what is known as the liberal international order (LIO). Di Maggio (2019: 341) notes that the LIO was characterised by "democratic peace theory and idealism" to which Western political leaders, including successive US presidents, were committed, involving the pursuit of human rights, democracy, the rule of law, and religious freedom. The LIO was pursued under American leadership for most of the period following World War II. The Trump presidency diverged from this well-trodden path: it sought to reshape America's foreign policy in line with the objectives of neo-nationalism, which the president claimed were in America's national interest. LIO goals were now decidedly secondary – if not downright irrelevant. Christian nationalist influence was apparent in relation to two of the Trump administration's foreign policy goals: prioritisation of international religious freedom and conservative social goals in the Global South, including severely restricting abortion availability by withholding funds to those countries which had a liberal policy in this regard (Haynes, 2020a).

In line with President Trump's neo-nationalism, US international relations during his presidency reflected concerns present in the country's domestic culture wars. Two facets of the latter were salient: abandonment of US support for the post–World War II LIO and less support for a universalist human rights regime (Bob, 2019a). Instead, under the foreign leadership of Secretary of State Pompeo, the USA pursued a particularistic policy, moulded by Christian nationalism, to champion international religious freedom above other human rights.

These were major changes to US foreign policy which for decades had pursued objectives that transcended the ideological preferences of both Republican and Democratic administrations. Following World War II and during the Cold War, successive US presidents sought to further America's role as 'the leader of the free world'. The USA claimed an international leadership role via involvement in universal organisations built on extensive international cooperation, notably the United Nations (UN). America's goal remained constant over time: to spread and disseminate America's perceived core values: democracy, human rights, religious freedom, and tariff-free international trade. Such goals were believed to be not only good for America but also appropriate for the rest of the world: they reflected the qualities which facilitated the USA's claim to be leader of the 'free world'. President Trump changed the policy, promising to "make America great again" by following the self-interested national interest policies exclusively.

It is important to stress what a sea change this was in American foreign policy. Since World War I, many Americans, including the then president, Woodrow Wilson, "viewed national self-determination as one of the building blocks of a new, more humane global order" (Lind, 2001). Wiebe (2002: 1) notes, however, that "disillusionment after the First World War turned to revulsion after the Second, and at mid-century Western intellectuals dug in to battle the nationalist spirit" (Wiebe, 2002: 1). As World War II drew to a close and it was clear that Nazi Germany was bound for defeat, America became a pillar of the emergent UN, a key supporter of the organisation's universalist human rights approach. The outcome of World War II was crucial for the global advance of human rights, seen after the war as a key international priority, especially in the context of decolonisation and the West's Cold War with the Soviet Union and international communism. At this time,

> the United States dropped its historic support for national self-determination, partly from a sense that German National Socialism, Italian fascism, and Japanese imperialism had discredited nationalism, but mainly out of a fear of instability that might be exploited by the communist bloc.
>
> (Lind, 2001)

During the Cold War, America sought to project the values of both liberal democracy and of its Christian civilisation in contrast to what it claimed was the Soviet Union's godless communism.

Prior to the Trump administration, the George W. Bush (2001–2009) and Barack Obama (2009–2017) presidencies continued with the traditional policies of strong US support for human rights, democracy, and gender equality. President Trump's priorities were different (Bettiza, 2019: 223). According to Ziv, Graham, and Cao (2019), the Trump administration's preference for "America First implies a definitive turning away from the United Nations, part of a wider strategy to achieve America's foreign policy goals by reducing dependence on international cooperation". Trump's America First foreign policy privileged the singular pursuit of America's goals seemingly unimpeded by internationalist commitments. The USA's foreign policy priorities included a turning away from international efforts to tackle the climate emergency as well as reducing its role in helping resolve humanitarian crises in various countries. The Trump administration's scepticism about the value of working collectively with international organisations to achieve collective goals was not however limited to the UN. It also informed US relations with other international and regional organisations, including the European Union, the North Atlantic Treaty Organization and America's partners in the North American Free Trade Association, Canada and Mexico. Overall, President Trump's America First foreign policy demonstrated that in his view international commitments were often undesirable, while globalisation is not good for the USA: Trump claimed repeatedly that 'globalism' was detrimental to America's national interests (Ziv, Graham, and Cao, 2019; Haynes, 2019a)

Like an earlier president, Andrew Jackson (1829–1837), the Trump administration's foreign policy approach was populist in the sense that it sought to pursue goals which many Americans believed were appropriate, including side-lining the UN and not attempting to export democracy and development via foreign aid (Moran, 2021: 367). According to Russell Mead (2010), populist nationalists such as President Trump hold the opinion that the fundamental government priority is to protect "the physical security and economic well-being of the American people in their national home". American diplomat and historian George Kennan asserted that it was vitally important for America's national interest to combat communism globally to protect the USA's international position. In 1948, Kennan wrote, in a manner reminiscent of Donald Trump nearly three-quarters of a century later:

> We [the US] have about 50% of the world's wealth but only 6.3% of its population. In this situation, we cannot fail to be the object of envy and resentment. Our real task in the coming period is to devise a pattern of relationships which will permit us to maintain this position of disparity. To do so, we will have to dispense with all sentimentality and daydreaming . . . we need not deceive ourselves that we can afford today the luxury of altruism and world-benefaction. . . . We should cease to talk about vague and unreal objectives such as human rights, the raising of living standards, and democratization. The day is not far off when we are going to have to deal in straight power concepts. The less we are then hampered by idealistic slogans, the better.
>
> (Kennan quoted in DiMaggio, 2019: 345)

In 2020, the USA had an estimated 4.23% of the global population and 29.4% of global wealth (Desjardins, 2020). Since the late 1940s, the USA's share of global wealth has shrunk by more than four-tenths (from about 50% to 29.4% of the global total) and its share of the world's population has fallen by a third (from 6.3% to 4.23%). Bryant (2015) noted that by 2015 almost 60% of Americans felt that the country's power was on the wane. Undoubtedly still a leading global power in 2020, the USA was however strongly challenged – economically, diplomatically, and ideologically – by several countries, notably China, as well as others, including Russia, Turkey, and Iran. Perhaps in response to what was objectively a changing global picture, Trump employed language reminiscent of Kennan's in highlighting his administration's America First foreign policy priorities: the USA could "no longer afford" an "altruistic" approach to international relations by playing a lead role in the liberal international order, in pursuit of universal "human rights, the raising of [global] living standards, and democratization". Trump's inaugural address in January 2017 made clear his administration's foreign policy priorities: "From this moment on it's going to be America First. Every decision on trade, on taxes, on immigration, on foreign affairs, will be made to benefit American workers and American families". This reinforced his campaign message that "we are getting out of the nation-building business and instead focusing on creating stability in the world" (cited in Moran, 2021: 368).

The shift to an America First foreign policy occurred at a time when the post-1945 *Pax Americana*, "when the US used its power to shape and direct global events, was weakening" (Moran, 2021: 366). Walt (2011) claimed that the world was moving towards the end of the "American Era". Trump highlighted differing opinions of what should be the US global role in the 2020s. On the one hand, there were those who argued that the USA should continue to play the main global role in maintaining international peace and security – because it was strongly in America's national interests to do so. On the other hand, there were those who did believe it was not in the USA's national interest to continue in this role (Moran, 2021: 368). The Trump administration adopted the latter approach, while the opposition Democrats chose the former.

The America First foreign policy was reflected in the 2017 National Security Strategy (NSS), the first of Trump's presidency. The NSS made it clear that Trump prioritised an America First strategy over maintenance of the liberal international order. President Obama had expressed determination to pursue a "rules-based international order" via US leadership to promote "peace, security, and opportunity through stronger cooperation to meet global challenges". Trump's NSS put forward a different approach: "We will pursue this beautiful vision – a world of strong, sovereign and independent nations, each with its own cultures and dreams, thriving side-by-side in prosperity, freedom and peace" (Moran, 2021: 368–369). Trump's NSS committed America to "pursue bilateral trade and investment agreements with countries that commit to fair and reciprocal trade" (cited in Moran, 2021: 368) According to Moran, with the use of such language,

"Trump appeared to view the world in terms of zero-sum interactions, not the multilateralism of the Liberal International Order whose supporters had argued that it guaranteed US security". Also published in 2017, the US Defense Department's *National Defense Strategy* (NDS, 2017) portrayed a similar world to that in the NSS: increasing anarchy and global disorder, "characterized by decline in the long-standing rules-based international order – creating a security environment more complex and volatile than any we have experienced in recent memory" (Moran, 2021: 368–369).

The Obama administration both was globalist in orientation and sought to build bridges with the Muslim world, which were in bad shape following 9/11 and the subsequent American-led invasions of Afghanistan and Iraq, both Muslim-majority countries. President Obama's overtures to the Muslim world after 9/11 were explicit recognition that while the 9/11 attackers were all Muslims, this did not mean that all Muslims were America's enemy. The Trump administration took a different approach both to America's global role and to the country's relationship with many Muslim-majority countries. With the defeat of the Islamic State in 2017 via an intensive bombing campaign led by the USA, President Trump's security focus remained on 'radical Islamic terrorism', although now the target was to deter Islamic terrorism at home via lone wolf attacks. The second facet of a new security orientation was on 'inter-state strategic competition', which became the primary concern of American national security. In particular, Russia and China were seen as the main challenges to America's continued prosperity and security. In the Middle East, Iran was judged to be the primary threat to America's main allies in the Middle East: Israel, Saudi Arabia, and the United Arab Emirates (Moran, 2021: 373].

Despite multiple challenges, for Trump and many Americans, the United States remains a world leader. Whereas after the Cold War, the United States played a key role in international 'democracy promotion' and sought to disseminate America's democratic ideals around the world, the Trump administration saw things differently. Rather than democracy, the Trump administration sought to spread another set of values: America's core 'civilisational' values which, reflecting the influence of Christian nationalism, focused on protecting the religious freedom of Christians, especially in 'unfriendly' Muslim countries in the Middle East. This policy was led by Secretary of State Pompeo and supported by Vice President Pence and Attorney General Barr, all of whom believed in the importance of disseminating America's 'Christian values' to societies and countries around the world.

To conclude this section, the Trump administration's America First foreign policy was a major, even a fundamental, change to the consistent international objectives of the USA following World War II. The defeat of

Nazism and fascism ushered in an era of championing Western values – including democracy and universal human rights – via the United Nations. The Trump administration had different strategic priorities and foreign policy goals, especially in relation to countries with differing cultures and civilisations, such as China and Iran. In the next section of the chapter, we turn attention to a key area of foreign policy divergence between the USA and many other Western countries: human rights, with a focus on international religious freedom.

Human rights and international religious freedom: America's changing position

We saw in Chapters 2 and 3 that the public role of religion in the USA is a key area of discord, with different stances taken by many Christian conservatives compared to those adopted by secular and religiously liberal Americans. Such was also the case in America's foreign policy during the Trump administration. Bettiza (2019) explains that over time religion assumed an increasingly important foreign policy role for successive administrations, especially from the time of the Reagan presidency in the 1980s. Bettiza argues that American foreign policy and what he calls "religious forces" became ever more inextricably entangled in the post-1980s, coinciding with a widespread religious resurgence in many parts of the world, including to some degree the most secular of regions, Western Europe (Bettiza, 2019). According to Bettiza, at this time in the USA boundaries between religion and state were redefined through processes of desecularisation. In relation to American foreign policy, this was evidenced in the Trump administration's attempts to reshape international relations in accord with its preference for a Christianised polity, in effect a preference for Christian nationalist values in the USA's international relations. This section examines the role of Christian nationalism in US foreign policy during the Trump presidency. It focuses on the international religious freedom policy of the Trump administration, championed by Secretary of State Pompeo, as a key example of the wider attempt to inject 'Christian values' into the administration's policies, in line with the goals of Christian nationalism.

The International Religious Freedom Act of 1998

Unlike many other Western countries, the USA has for decades prioritised religious freedom, both at home and in foreign policy. This is because whereas other Western countries have undergone prolonged periods of significant secularisation, which led to substantial declines in the public role of religion, the USA continues to be a religious country. This is evidenced by the fact that as many as 40% of Americans regularly attend religious services, much higher than any other Western country, especially in Western Europe. International religious freedom (IRF) has long been of great significance for American foreign policy. In America, IRF is a key concern for both religious and secular human rights advocacy groups (Haynes, 2008). IRF became of particular concern in the 1990s, a period of egregious trampling on many religious minorities' human rights in several countries, including North Korea and Sudan. The then president, Bill Clinton, initially seemed indifferent to the issue (Bettiza, 2019). This was not necessarily because his administration believed the issue to be unimportant but because he did not believe that it was an issue which needed prioritising in US foreign policy. Seeking to change the administration's view, an alliance of human rights advocacy groups successfully lobbied Congress and other arms of government, urging the Clinton administration to take IRF seriously.

Following intensive lobbying, President Clinton signed into law the International Religious Freedom Act (IRFA) in 1998.[1] The act identified international religious freedom as a core facet of America's foreign policy and from this time successive administrations pursued the policy, often with vigour. The Trump administration's policy on IRF is characterised both by great enthusiasm and by a distinctive ideological position, linked to Christian nationalism (Haynes, 2020b; Casey, 2017, 2020). This ideological focus became especially clear from April 2018, when Mike Pompeo was appointed as secretary of state. Pompeo, an evangelical Christian, applied Christian nationalist perspective to America's IRF policy, which endorsed Pompeo's personal view that religious freedom is primary among human rights (Casey, 2017, 2020; Stewart, 2020). Mainstream human rights advocacy groups, both religious and secular, viewed Pompeo's approach with alarm. While they did not question the goal of enhanced international religious freedom, they did question Pompeo's Christian nationalist approach (Verma, 2020).

As stated in the 1788 Constitution, religious freedom is a foundational component of US culture and values. During World War II, the US government portrayed the 'Christian' West's fight against fascism/Nazism as an international struggle between 'good' and 'evil'. In 1948, leading American Christians, notably the then first lady, Eleanor Roosevelt, were instrumental in crafting the Universal Declaration of Human Rights (UDHR), a fundamental document of the United Nations.[2] During the Cold War, America's ideological battle with the Soviet Union emphasised the USA's Christian culture and the USSR's 'Godless' one (Glendon, 2010). After the Cold War, US foreign policy prioritised decolonisation, democracy, human rights, and anti–slavery and human trafficking. As already noted, promulgation of international religious freedom was the motive for the 1998 IRFA. While in the early

2000s, both Bush and Obama administrations pursued IRF policies with "an implicit Christian soft spot", the Trump presidency prioritised "attention to Christian concerns and communities" which became "even more overt and explicit" (Bettiza, 2019: 223).

The 1998 IRFA was the result of bipartisan efforts. It was the outcome of a consensual effort to persuade an initially indifferent administration to take international religious freedom seriously. An ideologically varied group of religious human rights advocacy groups were instrumental in helping create a new architecture for human rights' monitoring and advocacy in American foreign policy (Green., Rozell, and Wilcox, 2003; Hertzke, 2006; Haynes, 2008). Hertzke (2006) explains that it involved an "unlikely alliance" comprising Protestant Evangelicals, conservative Catholics, mainline Protestants, progressive Catholics, Jews, Copts, Buddhists, Baha'is, Jehovah's Witnesses, and Scientologists. All agreed that "religious freedom [w]as a neglected norm that needed greater attention" (Bettiza, 2019: 65–66). The alliance's lobbying was successful due to a shift "from a particularist Christocentric discourse to a more universalistic religious freedom one [that] was pivotal in ensuring that a controversial act", which authorised the State Department "to be systematically involved in global religious matters" and received Congress's undivided approval and President Clinton's assent (Bettiza, 2019: 65).

Following IRFA, three related acts were passed in five years (2000–2004):

- *The Trafficking Victims Protection Act* (2000): The act targeted international crime syndicates who sent children and women, mainly from the Global South, into prostitution and sweatshops in many parts of the world (Lobasz, 2019)
- *The Sudan Peace Act* (2002): Christian evangelicals championed the act, outraged by Sudan's then Islamist government's persecution of southern Sudanese Christians and animists. The act and its accompanying sanctions were influential in helping to develop the road map for Sudan's ceasefire (2003) and subsequent peace treaty (2004) (Srinivasan, 2014)
- *The North Korea Human Rights Act* (2004): Christian evangelicals and Korean Americans strongly lobbied for this act. It encouraged the Bush administration both to aid North Korean defectors and to draw attention to its government's egregious human rights violations and nuclear weapons programme (Chang, 2006)

Collectively, the three acts focused on two globally relevant issues – human trafficking and slavery – and two specific country-based concerns: persecution of Sudan's religious minorities and, in North Korea, absolute denial of religious freedom and a more general refusal to recognise most human rights. The acts highlighted two attributes of the "unlikely alliance" referred to earlier. The first was the strong interfaith consensus which transcended conventional particularist interest group politics, bringing together in pursuit of a common goal even though their religious positions were different. The second attribute was the alliance's strong support for the Bush and Obama administrations' international concern with minorities' human rights. During the former, there was sustained support for females' rights in Afghanistan and a wide-ranging and high-profile HIV/AIDS programme: the President's Emergency Plan for AIDS Relief (PEPFAR) (McAlister, 2019). In short, the acts were the result of interfaith efforts, involving both conservative and liberal religious groups from mainstream Christianity and minority faiths.

The Obama administration's foreign policy supported a wide range of human rights, including for sexual minorities, such as LGBTQ+ (lesbian, gay, bisexual, transgender, and questioning/queer) individuals and communities (Cooper, 2015; McAlister, 2019; Marsden, 2020). During the Obama presidency, IRFA was strengthened by two new pieces of legislation: the Near East and South Central Asia Religious Freedom Act (2014), whose terms included a new regional special advisor for religious minorities, and the Frank R. Wolf International Religious Freedom Act (2016), known as 'the Wolf Act'. The Wolf Act required (1) the executive to compose and announce a Special Watch List for countries which seemed to the US government to be significantly denying religious freedom to significant numbers of their citizens, and (2) compilation of both 'Entities of Particular Concern' and 'Designated Persons' lists. These were aimed at non-state actors, notably the Islamic State, at the time egregiously abusing many persons' religious freedom in territory it briefly controlled. In addition, the Wolf Act committed the State Department to an online training course on IRF for all foreign service officers (Marsden, 2020: 4). In sum, over time additional measures were added to IRFA in order to strengthen and deepen US commitment to IRF, including in relation to females and sexual minorities' human rights.

The creation and execution of IRFA took place in the context of a consensual and bipartisan approach to international religious freedom, involving a wide alliance of many faith groups, which applied itself through three presidencies: those of Clinton, Bush, and Obama. All were characterised by what Bettiza (2019) calls a "Christocentric approach". On the other hand, each was ideologically flexible enough to accommodate a range of concerns, including anti-AIDS and pro-LGBTQ+ policies, a focus on particular regions of especial concern such as the Near East and South-Central Asia, as well as serious efforts to try to protect Muslim minorities in, for example, Afghanistan and Pakistan.

The next section explains that the Trump administration's approach to IRF was a much more partisan approach which strongly favoured particularist Christian nationalist goals.

Christian nationalism and international religious freedom

The US policy on international religious freedom has been extensively surveyed. Farr's (2008) summary of the moral and ethical desirability of IRF is a thoughtful analysis which commands wide attention.[3] He argues that promoting religious freedom around the world is not just a good thing in itself. It is also a necessary component of a foreign policy which aims to be both just and ethical. Hurd (2015) regards America's IRF policy as designed to aid the USA's bid for international hegemony, via an "approved list" of religious minorities which the USA would seek to assist, but with less obvious concern for those not on the list. Moreover, Hurd (2015: 5, 35) argues that, globally, protections for the rights of religious minorities have "gone viral" and "the good religion-bad religion mandate has become an industry". Joustra (2016) claims that what Hurd is dissatisfied with is not "religion, or religious freedom, but really with the project of liberalism". That is, for Hurd, Joustra claims, protection of religious freedom around the world is a project of liberalism, along with other human rights such as democracy, equality, and the rights of minorities.

In June 2020, President Trump issued Executive Order 13,926 referring to IRF as a moral and national security issue:

> Religious freedom, America's first freedom, is a moral and national security imperative. Religious freedom for all people worldwide is a foreign policy priority of the United States, and the United States will respect and vigorously promote this freedom. As stated in the 2017 National Security Strategy, our Founders understood religious freedom not as a creation of the state, but as a gift of God to every person and a right that is fundamental for the flourishing of our society.
>
> (Federal Register, 2020)

President Trump's comments in the quotation underline that religious freedom is a core concern of his administration's foreign policy, which he believes is granted not by governments but "as a gift of God".[4] However, unlike Joustra (2016), Philpott (2020), Barker (2020), and Casey (2020), President Trump asserts the paramountcy of religious freedom ("America's first freedom") over all other human rights. Trump affirms that if foreign governments deny religious freedom to their citizens, then the USA "will respect and vigorously promote this freedom". The notion that human rights are a creation of God, not of humans, is a core belief of Christian nationalism (Haynes, 2019a, 2020a). This section examines the claim that the Trump administration used IRF policy not only to pursue and further Christian nationalist goals but also to emphasise certain Christians' religious freedom only, which, perhaps unintentionally, undermined those of many females and the human rights of sexual minorities.

Philpott welcomes Trump's support of international religious freedom, especially the claim that it "is a moral and national security imperative". Philpott points to recent killings of "several hundred Christians . . . killed in Nigeria", China's "brutal crackdown on churches", and incarceration of "a million Uighur Muslims", and the "high" or "very high" multi-faith religious restrictions on religion in around 50 other countries. These moral issues are augmented by concerns for US national security. "Religious freedom mitigates terrorism and civil war, strengthens democracy, enhances economic development, fosters peace, enables reconciliation and advances opportunities for women" (Philpott, 2020). Barker underlines Philpott's concern with widespread multi-faith religious restrictions in numerous countries. Religious persecution "target[s] the most vulnerable, particularly religious minorities, non-believers, converts from the majority religion, and those who otherwise dissent from or reject the religious establishment". Further, there are many other threats to religious freedom, including "technology-enabled state repression of religion, non-state violence aided by inept governance, and blasphemy and apostasy laws that are regularly weaponized against religious minorities or dissenters". To try to deal with any or all of these threats, "new forms of [international] cooperation" are essential (Barker, 2020; author's interview #2).

Shaun Casey (2017), special representative for religion and global affairs at the Department of State during the Obama presidency, agrees that there are moral and national security concerns encouraging the US government to seek improved global religious freedom. Casey contends, however, that under President Trump, "[e]ngagement with religious actors and communities has dissolved from the global, inclusive, strategy of the previous [Obama] administration to an almost exclusively conservative Christian, primarily Protestant, engagement" (author's interview #9). As already mentioned, this is also a concern noted by Bettiza (2019: 223).

During the Trump presidency, IRF policy was strongly influenced by Christian nationalist values and beliefs (Stewart, 2020; Sherratt, 2019; Bump, 2019; Verma, 2020). Christian nationalist values and beliefs are however contested; there is not a single set of such values and beliefs that all would agree constitutes their core (Gaston, 2019). Altshuler (2016) claims that they derive from an acceptance that culturally, socially, and politically, US principles and achievements reflect "fundamental values of

Western society that are believed to come from both Judaism and Christianity".

Critics contend, however, that Christian nationalist values and beliefs privilege certain groups' religious freedom over others' human rights. Central to Christian nationalist understandings of the world are the congruence of Jewish and Christian values and beliefs, referred to as Judeo-Christian values. Jews for a Secular Democracy[5] note the current prevalence of references to "Judeo-Christian values", including among Christian conservative groups, such as Focus on the Family (FOTF), whose public policy focus is self-described as "drawn from the wisdom of the Bible and the Judeo-Christian ethic". Under this guise of Judeo-Christian values, FOTF opposes same-sex marriage and LGBTQ equality, staunchly lobbies against abortion and reproductive freedom, and promotes creationism and abstinence-only sex education (Jews for a Secular Democracy, 2019).[6]

These comments emphasise that in the USA and many other countries, human rights debates take place in a polarised political, social, and cultural climate (Haynes, 2017, 2019b). Bob argues that such discourses have "great utility in political conflict". The rights involved are not necessarily the essential objectives over which opposing entities compete. Bob emphasises that they "fight over a wide range of substantive demands and hope that using rights-oriented discourses could reinforce their political interests" (Bob, 2019a: 16). This suggests that, because many understandings of rights are influenced by political and ideological considerations, the language of rights is used to try to achieve proponents' objectives. The latter are not necessarily concerned only with rights but may also involve additional political, social, and/or cultural objectives (Schwartz, 2019).

The Trump administration paid great attention to an issue of great importance to Judeo-Christian beliefs: strong support for Israel. In addition, Judeo-Christian values include more generally strong defence of religious freedom both at home and abroad. The Trump administration has shown itself to be enthusiastic in this regard, targeting, *inter alia*, communist states (China, Vietnam, North Korea) and several Muslim-majority countries (including Pakistan and Turkey). The US focus is on Muslim Uighurs and Tibetan Buddhists (China) and religious minorities, including Ahmadis and Alevis (Pakistan and Turkey).[7] In sum, the Trump administration highlights persecution of several groups, including Christians and non-mainstream Muslims (Philpott, 2020; Barker, 2020).

These examples underline that the Trump administration actively and strongly pursued international religious freedom in its foreign policy. The administration did not restrict itself to seeking to protect Christians from persecution but, like earlier administrations, sought to extend its protection to non-Christian religious minorities, for example, Uighurs in China and

Alevis in Turkey. Seeking to protect religious minorities was not a new approach for US foreign policy; what was novel was the Trump administration's privileging of Christian nationalist values. Unlike earlier administrations, the Trump presidency's approach was contoured by ideological commitment to a Judeo-Christian worldview. It replaced a more flexible Christocentric approach, which characterised the administrations of Presidents Clinton, Bush, and Obama and reflects the rise to prominence of Christian nationalism.

Strong supporters of Christian nationalist goals, such as Tony Perkins, head of Family Research Council, congratulated the Trump administration for its exemplary commitment to advancing international religious freedom. Critics saw things differently: the injection of Christian nationalism into foreign policy was seen significantly to undermine the rights of women and sexual minorities. Secretary of State Pompeo was a key figure in the Trump administration's IRF policy. Pompeo established three initiatives on IRF during 2018–2020; all were informed by the values of Christian nationalism: the Commission on Unalienable Rights, the annual Ministerial on Advancing Religious Freedom, and the International Religious Freedom Alliance (Haynes, 2020a). Christian nationalist principles were invoked from the 1776 Declaration of Independence. Critics feared that international human rights, developed over the decades since the Universal Declaration of Human Rights (1948) under UN auspices, would fundamentally change under Pompeo's direction, including females' and sexual minorities' rights.

Concern was also fuelled by one of the early acts of the Trump administration: to reinstitute the so-called Mexico City policy, also known as the global gag rule. This stops US government support for international family planning programmes that "perform, promote or offer information about abortion". In addition, the Trump administration worked industriously at the UN to remove all references to "sexual and reproductive health", the term preferred by mainstream human rights activists (Bob, 2019b). Several Trump administration appointees worked internationally to insert anti-LGBTQ views into USA policy. For example, at the 2019 Commission on the Status of Women (CSW) at the UN, the US delegation attempted to remove "gender-responsive" language from CSW exit documents. US Ambassador at the UN, Cherith Norman Chalet, stated in a speech at the event, "we are not about gender jargon . . . we are about women and girls". Some saw this as an effort to weaken the rights of non-binary individuals, in line with the Trump administration's broader attacks on the LGBTQ community (Ford, 2019; Verma, 2020; author's interview #7).

Concerns about the rights of women and LGBTQ+ communities were not restricted to events at the UN. A chief US ally, Poland, held a presidential election in early July 2020. The winner was Andrzej Duda, a vociferous critic of LGBTQ+ rights, who narrowly triumphed over Rafal Trzaskowski, the liberal mayor of Warsaw. During his presidency, Duda pledged to "defend children from LGBT ideology". Duda is a friend and ally of President Trump (FP Editors, 2019). Pompeo restated his opposition to same-sex marriage in July 2018 during his confirmation hearing before the Senate Foreign Relations Committee. Sarah Kate Ellis, president and CEO of the LGBTQ+ rights group GLAAD, stated that Pompeo's hostility

> to marriage equality and LGBTQ rights further proves that he is dangerously wrong to serve as our nation's chief diplomat. . . . His personal ties to anti-LGBTQ hate groups and clear refusal to support the hard-fought equal rights of the LGBTQ community make him wholly unqualified to promote human rights abroad.
> (Brammer, 2018)

Finally, Gevisser remarks that in the course of

> his presidency, Donald Trump has rolled back transgender rights as part of his efforts to consolidate his conservative Evangelical base, for whom 'gender ideology' has become the new evil; the latest bulwark against assaults on 'the family' now that same-sex marriage was legal and supported by a majority of Americans.
> (Gevisser quoted in Tóibín, 2020; see also Gevisser, 2020)

Conclusion

This chapter surveyed the Trump administration's neo-nationalist approach to international relations. It examined the Trump administration's foreign policy links to America First nationalism and Christian nationalism. A recent Pew Research Center survey indicates that many Americans believe that there was an increase in discriminatory behaviour in the USA during the Trump presidency. For example, the "public has negative views of the country's racial progress; more than half say Trump has made race relations worse" (Pew Research Center, 2019). It can be hypothesised that the Trump administration's religious freedom policy encourages the rise of hate crimes and hostility toward some minority faiths in America, as well as to exacerbate tensions over religion, race, and ethnicity internationally (for example, Trump's strong support for Israel) (Haynes, 2019a: 141, 170). It is also relevant to examine and probe international religious leaders' responses to the Trump administration's Judeo-Christian approach and to consider how such policies have been received by human rights advocacy groups in countries experiencing religious conflict or the oppression of religious minorities (for example, China, Russia, Myanmar, Syria, Yemen, Pakistan, Turkey) (Haynes, 2020a). While the current chapter does not examine these issues due to lack of space, their examination suggests a fruitful avenue for future research.

The controversial issue of the USA's approach to international religious freedom was highlighted when President Trump appeared clutching a Bible – upside down – outside St. John's Episcopal church in Washington DC on 1 June 2020 in the aftermath of the death of an African-American, George Floyd, killed by a white police officer. The Right Rev. Mariann Budde, the Episcopal bishop of Washington, accused the president of using the church for a photo opportunity and expressed outrage that law enforcement dispersed the crowd of overwhelmingly peaceful demonstrators proclaiming that "Black Lives Matter" (Boorstein and Bailey, 2020). Their response makes it plain that not all American Christians are united in supporting Trump's Christian nationalist-influenced religious freedom policies at home.

Turning to foreign policy, two policy innovations from Secretary of State Pompeo – the annual Ministerial on Advancing Religious Freedom and the International Religious Freedom Alliance – bring together many countries which see eye to eye with the Trump administration in terms of its particular approach to international religious freedom. On the one hand, the International Religious Freedom Alliance purports to champion international religious freedom in general. But what of the US government's attack on China over its government's treatment of the Muslim Uighur minority? While this issue is not about the plight of Christians, it does concern a country – China – that is a key global rival of the USA. To attack its government over its treatment of a religious minority fulfils two goals: (1) critiques China in an area in which it is vulnerable, and (2) indicates the USA's foreign policy commitment to minorities' religious (and cultural) freedom. For the Trump administration's domestic support base, the anti-China policy highlights that the USA is willing to 'take on' egregious deniers of 'religious freedom' such as China, while also implicitly castigating the country's government for its denial of human rights more generally. A particularistic approach to religious freedom and human rights is also shown in the case of the Trump administration's relationship with the rulers of Saudi Arabia. Among the world's most egregious deniers of the rights of religious minorities, including Christians, the Saudi government is not publicly criticised by the Trump administration for its approach, unlike its approach to China's denials of religious and cultural freedom to the Uighurs. Instead, the importance to the Trump administration of the Saudi government's role regionally – that is, its anti-Iran, anti-radical political changes, pro-stability stances – easily takes precedence over any IRF concerns that the administration has over the Saudi government's treatment of religious minorities (Fox, 2016: 126, 131). In conclusion, it would appear that the Trump administration's America First approach to international relations furthers self-interested goals which draw on the beliefs of Christian Nationalists regarding human rights and religious freedom.

Notes

1 IRFA aims "To condemn violations of religious freedom, and to promote, and to assist other governments in the promotion of, the fundamental right to freedom of religion" (https://uscode.house.gov/view.xhtml?path=/prelim@title22/chapter73&edition=prelim).
2 Roosevelt served as First Lady of the United States from 4 March 1933 to 12 April 1945, during her husband President Franklin D. Roosevelt's four terms in office. She was the longest-serving First Lady of the United States. Roosevelt was chair of the United Nations Human Rights Commission, instrumental in the creation of the UDHR. Roosevelt was a lifelong Protestant Christian, a member of the Episcopalian church, and regularly attended church services (Glendon, 2010).
3 In 1999, Thomas Farr became the first director of the State Department's Office of International Religious Freedom. Currently (December 2020), he is president of the Religious Freedom Institute, an NGO working to achieve worldwide acceptance of religious freedom (www.religiousfreedominstitute.org/).
4 Martin Castro, appointed by President Obama to chair the US Commission on Civil Rights, writes that *religious freedom* is often used as a "code word" for "discrimination, intolerance, racism, sexism, homophobia, Islamophobia," and "Christian supremacy" (Peaceful Coexistence, 2016: 30).
5 "Jews for a Secular Democracy is a pluralistic initiative of the Society for Humanistic Judaism" (https://jfasd.org/2019/10/why-judeo-christian-values-are-problematic/).
6 James Dobson, founder and head of FOTF, is a strong supporter of President Trump (Dobson, 2019). Dobson is also a friend and ideological ally of Secretary of State Pompeo. See Dobson's 2020 interview with Pompeo at www.state.gov/secretary-michael-r-pompeo-with-dr-james-dobson-of-family-talk-with-james-dobson/ We refer to this interview in the conclusion of this article.
7 For details, see USCIRF's annual reports at: www.uscirf.gov/reports-briefs/annual-report.

5 Conclusion
Donald Trump and neo-nationalism in America, 2016–2020

This concluding chapter is divided into two sections, followed by an epilogue. The latter follows the presidential election result of 3 November 2020, which saw President Donald Trump ejected from office through the clear wishes of a majority of Americans who voted. Trump received nearly eight million votes fewer than his rival, Joe Biden. In addition, Biden received a clear majority of Electoral College votes, leading to his inauguration as the 46th president on 20 January 2021.

This concluding chapter reflects on the four years of Donald Trump's presidency, during which he projected the ideology of neo-nationalism in order to receive and maintain the support of both Christian nationalists and America First nationalists.

Neo-nationalism and the Trump administration

The outcome of the 3 November 2020 presidential election was a clear victory for Joe Biden. It was also evidence that Donald Trump's victory in the 2016 presidential election was not a fluke: more than 70 million Americans voted for Trump in 2020, a substantial increase on the number of votes he received in 2016 (nearly 63 million). The overall turnout – at around 67.5%– was the highest in a century and it illustrated importance that tens of millions of Americans attached to the outcome of the poll.

Neo-nationalism as practised by President Trump is an ideology which trumpets the perceived superiority of Judeo-Christian values and beliefs over others. Neo-nationalism had strong electoral appeal among Christian nationalists in America. The claim of this book is that Donald Trump was able successfully to draw on the concerns of two constituencies – Christian nationalists and America First nationalists – to win the presidential election in November 2016. Over the next four years, he filled his administration with supportive appointees and sought a fundamental realignment of America's direction, both at home and abroad. At home, the aim was to reward his supporters, both religious and secular, by bringing in policies which they believed would advance their interests. For Christian nationalists, the main win was appointing conservative justices to the Supreme Court in order to try to facilitate the spread of Judeo-Christian values in relation to the rights of women, sexual minorities, and children's education. The focus was on America's supposed 'Christian foundations' which Christian nationalists regard as fundamental to the country's well-being, stability, and security. America First nationalists, on the other hand, may have been less concerned about religious freedom and more encouraged by the claims of President Trump that he was the only leader who could 'make America great again'. He would do this, he claimed, by wielding America's power exclusively for self-interest in international relations. At home he would quell illegal – and unwanted – immigration of Mexicans and others from Central America, block the entry of Islamic terrorists into the USA, and bring home millions of jobs that China, Mexico, and other competitor countries had unfairly and unjustly 'stolen'.

During his 2016 presidential election campaign, Trump surrounded himself with nationalists, including Stephen Miller, Stephen K. Bannon, and Sebastian Gorka. Each was a short-term (Bannon, Gorka) or long-term member of his administration (Miller). These men share an understanding that the USA is engaged in a culture war between nativists and globalists. Miller is Trump's chief speechwriter and is credited with authoring the president's 'American carnage' inaugural address. He has been a key adviser since the early days of Trump's presidency and was a chief architect of Trump's executive order restricting Muslim immigration from several countries. Few on the hard-right thought he needed to offer any clarification or qualification for this policy.[1] Guerrero (2020) describes Miller as the architect of Trump's border and immigration policies, helping Trump "conjure an invasion of animals to come steal American jobs and spill American blood".

Stephen Bannon is a former White House chief strategist, past Breitbart[2] chief, and leader of a putative populist far-right international movement, 'The Movement'. "Bannon helped get Stephen Miller into the Trump administration, and Bannon was another one of Stephen Miller's mentors" (Guerrero, 2020). Bannon was a key adviser during the first nine months of the presidency of Donald Trump. He was ousted from this role in August 2017, following infighting in the White House involving Trump's son-in-law and senior advisor, Jared Kushner. Despite losing his job with the Trump administration, Bannon is an influential figure on the far-right both in the USA and internationally. He regards himself as an ideologue, a key proponent of the Trump administration's America First agenda. Bannon believes that America's foundational values are rooted in nativist ethics and principles (Tondo, 2018).

Bannon is both an economic nationalist and nativist, an admirer of several right-wing French ideologues and novelists, including Renaud Camus, who coined the phrase "The Great Replacement", and Jean Raspail, author of a 1973 novel, *The Camp of the Saints*. Camus refers to what he understands as a "plot" to replace ethnic French people with Muslim migrants. In his 2012 book, *The Great Replacement*, which echoes the concerns of Raspail's earlier book, Camus writes of the conspiracy theory that native French Catholics, and Christian Europeans more generally, will eventually be completely sidelined and substituted by waves of immigrants from North Africa, the Middle East, and sub-Saharan Africa. This theory found a ready home among prominent right-wing nationalists in the USA, such as Richard Spencer (Malice, 2018). Raspail's ideas are at the root of the 'identitarian' doctrine, which claims that globalisation will create an undesirable homogeneous culture, with disappearing distinct national and/or cultural identities. An alternative, 'true pluralism' or 'ethnopluralism' would imply separation of races. These ideas are said to have influenced both "Steve Bannon at Breitbart and the American white supremacist leader Richard Spencer" (Jones, 2018).

While Bannon is not generally perceived as someone especially influenced by Christian beliefs, Donald Trump was. As already noted, Trump was a massively popular choice for president of most white Christian conservatives in 2016 and again in 2020. In both elections, he gained the support of more than 80% of this constituency. It is unlikely that such support was due to Trump's "character, story, agenda, or candidacy" which does not seem to be well aligned with

> Scripture, the cross, the gospel, or personal/social transformation (Bebbington's evangelical markers in simple terms). However, his "Make America Great Again" slogan, along with his maligning of women, immigrants, and all "losers" while triumphantly holding up a Bible, fits Christianism perfectly.
>
> (Jethani, 2016)

The ideology of what Jethani calls "Christianism" (or Christian nationalism) is not unique to Trump. Instead, as we have noted in this book, recent years have seen right-wing populist politicians not only in the USA but also in Europe, Brazil, Australia, and elsewhere take an idealised 'Christianity' as both a defining feature of national purity and an important component of neo-nationalism. However, as "with the idea of Islamism this has little, if any, theological depth to it, but it is the application of Christianity to a political ideology, one that establishes the pure people against outsiders" (Ryan, 2018).

Christian civilisationism draws inspiration from and has foundations in claimed 'Judeo-Christian' values. That is, the ideology of Christian civilisationism is rooted in a belief that, culturally, socially, and politically, US principles and achievements stem from the country's claimed Judeo-Christian values.[3] This view has been politically weaponised in recent years, with several racial and religious groups, notably "Mexicans" and "Muslims", vilified for their values and beliefs which are seen by Trump and many of his supporters as lesser than those of Judeo-Christianity. For example, former Republican congressman Steve King of Iowa called immigrants "dogs" and "dirt". In addition, Donald Trump "infamously declared that most immigrants crossing the southern border were 'rapists and criminals' and pledged to ban all Muslims from entering the US" (Siddiqui, 2019).

Trump's neo-nationalist electoral appeal was in part based upon his claim that not only "Mexicans" but also "Islam" and "Muslims" pose an existential threat to America and its civilisation. For figures such as Trump and King, Islam is a cultural, ideational, and emerging existential challenge to the US which must be defeated in order to ensure the purity of American culture. It requires policies both to limit the numbers of Muslims in the USA and to prevent the spread of *sharia* law, allegedly spearheaded by American representatives of the Muslim Brotherhood (Anti-Defamation League, 2013; Beydoun, 2018: 105–109).

Trump's rhetoric and policies were echoed in other parts of the world, notably Europe. There, in many regional countries, political ideologies of neo-nationalism – with their religious or cultural and secular national interest concerns – draw extensively on a claimed contrast between "liberal" and "illiberal" values. The former is exemplified by, for example, French civilisational values. France's president, Emmanuel Macron, suggested in July 2017 that Africa's problems are civilisationally rooted, a mix of security, social, and political issues. Macron claimed that Africa's "problems . . . are completely different" to those of Europe, as they are 'civilisational' and include "[f]ailed states, complex democratic transitions and extremely difficult demographic transitions. . . . Islamist terrorism, drugs and weapons trafficking" (Dearden, 2017). Macron's depiction of Africa highlights what he sees as the region's lack of "European-ness", that is, insufficient modernisation. According to Huntington (1996: 68; emphasis added),

> [m]odernization involves industrialization, urbanization, increasing levels of literacy, education, wealth, and social mobilization, and more complex and diversified occupational structures. . . . *The qualities that*

make a society Western, in contrast, are special: the classical legacy, Christianity, the separation of church and state, the rule of law, civil society.

While in Trump's rhetoric "Mexicans" take the place of Macron's "Africans", the sentiments expressed by both leaders are more or less identical: we cannot allow uncivilised foreigners with different – and inferior – values and beliefs from affecting the civilisational purity of our country. To do this runs the risk of fatally damaging our civilisational foundations, whether Christian (USA) or Republican (France).

Although the ideas of political scientist Samuel Huntington are not automatically associated with the beliefs of Emmanuel Macron or Donald Trump, they appear to share similar understandings of the world. For Huntington, being 'modern' and being 'Western' are different. That is, 'modernity' has generic qualities – including industrialisation, urbanisation, and higher levels of literacy, education, and wealth. Being 'Western', on the other hand, implies adhesion to a particularist civilisation ('the classical legacy') and religion ('Christianity'), with foundations in ubiquitous political and social institutions (that is, church-state separation, 'the rule of law', and independent civil societies). According to Macron, some non-Western civilisations, such as those in Africa, lack these attributes. Instead, the region is replete with "failed states", a lack of democracy, widespread Islamist terrorism, and extensive criminality. Macron sees these as the inescapable cultural and civilisational differences characterising the West and Africa respectively, and which explains the relative political, economic, and social stability and security of the former compared to the latter.

In Central Europe, neo-nationalists such as Viktor Orbán of Hungary seek to 'culturalise' religion and citizenship, to the detriment of Muslims and non-Christians, including in his case, Jews (author's interviews with #2, #3, #11, and #14). 'Culturalisation' refers to the necessary adaptation to or imposition of the culture of 'Christian' indigenes on the Other. According to Rogers Brubaker (2016), "the culturalization of religion is doubly convenient from a nationalist-populist point of view". This is for two main reasons. First, Christianity is thereby favoured as "*culture* in a way that it cannot be privileged *as religion*, given the liberal state's commitment to neutrality in religious matters". Second, "it allows minority religious practices, redefined as cultural, to be *restricted* in a way that would not otherwise be possible, given the liberal state's commitment to religious freedom" (emphases added).

The notion of irreducible cultural differences between native white Christian Americans and many others is a key claim of Donald Trump. It facilitated the hostility of his administration to Muslims, 'Mexicans', and countries of Haiti, El Salvador, and Africa. Trump referred to them as "shit-hole" countries during a closed-door meeting with congressional leaders and Cabinet members in January 2018. Yet, he may have unwittingly planted the seed for the unravelling of a critical part of his deportation agenda. In June 2018, the US District Court in San Francisco had its first hearing of a lawsuit challenging the Trump administration's revocation of Temporary Protected Status (TPS) for over 200,000 foreign nationals from four countries who currently live in the United States. The lawsuit alleged that Trump's rhetoric demonstrates that his administration's cancellation of TPS was motivated by bigotry, rather than policy concerns. Ahilan Arulanantham, legal director at the American Civil Liberties Union of Southern California and co-counsel for the plaintiffs, stated,

> The Trump administration's decision to end TPS for people from these countries was motivated by its racism against non-white, non-Europeans immigrants. That racist motivation was obvious from a number of statements that this president and others in the administration made, including about TPS holders specifically.
>
> (Woodhouse, 2018)

Brubaker (2017) argues that right-wing populists in both the USA and Europe have a "Christian civilisationist" worldview. This views "Islam" as the main threat to the indigenous society's "civilisational integrity". The proposed remedy is to counter the perceived threat to national integrity by use of a novel ideology: "Christianism", a self-conscious counterpoint to "Islamism". Christianism is characterised by overt, often extreme, anti-Islamism. It can include apparently liberal views on issues of gender and sexuality. They are used to seek to distinguish "enlightened", secularised European civilisation from allegedly regressive and repressive Islamic culture. This approach was adopted successfully by several prominent Dutch politicians, including the assassinated Pim Fortuyn, his ideological successor, Gert Wilders, and France's former president Nicholas Sarkozy. According to DeHanas and Shterin (2018: 178), the "same dynamics of Christian civilizationism are mirrored in many cases throughout Europe and in the U.S."

The recent political salience of Christianism is both manifested and exemplified by President Trump's words and deeds during both the 2016 presidential election campaign and the four years of his administration. The Trump presidency both stimulates and encourages Trump "wannabes' around the world, not only in Europe, such as Viktor Orbán in Hungary, but also elsewhere in the world, including Narendra Modi in India, Brazil's president, Jair Bolsonaro, and the prime minister of the UK, Boris Johnson

(Whitehead, Perry, and Baker, 2018). Ideological links between such leaders encourage what has been called 'Christianist internationalism'. It brings together a group of like-minded, values-based, nationalist politicians, united by shared dislikes: of Islam, liberalism, globalism, multiculturalism, and cosmopolitanism (Haynes, 2019a: 61–62). Trump's ideas about immigration and the necessity of keeping Muslims out of the USA has struck a chord with many such people. For example, Sebastian Kurz, Austria's chancellor, has thought out loud about a "Berlin-Rome-Vienna" axis to fight illegal immigration, and Richard Grenell, US ambassador to Germany in 2018–2020, sought to encourage Trump-style populist nationalists in Germany and other European countries (Stewart, 2020).

Neo-nationalism and immigration

In the chapters of this book, we have seen that many Americans, including Donald Trump, view Islam as a faith and Muslims as a people as undifferentiatedly linked to the violent events of 9/11 (Kamali, 2015). Trump was able to exploit fears of "Islamic terrorism" electorally. It encouraged him to push both for a "Muslim ban" and to claim the alleged superiority of 'Judeo-Christian' beliefs and values. Highlighting these concerns by Trump during his presidential campaign and his presidency allowed him to claim that Islam and Muslims are a key source of America's key travails, especially after 9/11. Overall, Trump's Christianity-orientated neo-nationalism enabled him to claim that what needed to be done to "make America great again" was to build on the foundations of America as a "Christian nation" by excluding or reducing the perceptions of worth of those of different religious and cultural persuasions.

While it is clear that anti-Muslim rhetoric was an important component of his worldview, it did not amount to the totality of his prejudices. An important aspect of Donald Trump's appeal for millions of Americans in both the 2016 and 2020 elections was his claim that he would severely curtail illegal immigration into America of people from countries that he implicitly claimed would not be "suitable" citizens of the USA.

A second key component of Trump's neo-nationalism was an apparent wish to keep the country as 'white' as possible and to deny entry into the country of those who did not satisfy the criteria in this regard. Trump's rhetoric consistently focused on "illegal" immigrants who were not only unwelcome because they "stole" American jobs but also because their cultures and behaviour were not allegedly conducive to American values. This component of Trump's neo-nationalism was not unique to the USA but was also found elsewhere where neo-nationalists were in power or seeking to be elected to government. For example, while not every major political concern that Europe has faced since the summer of 2015 has been linked to the international migration/refugee crisis, many have been. The unexpected, apparently uncontrollable influx of a million people arriving in Europe from Syria, Iraq, and elsewhere in the Middle East since 2015 demonstrably caused shockwaves to European politics and institutions. The crisis also caused major self-questioning in Europe, in a manner reminiscent of the fall of the Berlin Wall more than a quarter of a century ago: what is Europe, and what is its place in a fast-changing global context? Similar concerns animated many Americans for the same reasons as they concerned many Europeans: 'uncontrolled' immigration of numerous people with unacceptable or unwelcome cultural, religious, racial, or ethnic attributes would be societally damaging while threatening increased unemployment among indigenous workers as the new immigrants would be expected to take jobs at lower wages.

While in America, Donald Trump's approach to immigration was almost totally to see it as unwelcome – especially if immigrants came from "shithole" countries – in some European countries there was a different approach. Rather than seeking to appeal to neo-nationalist prejudices, in Germany Chancellor Angela Merkel's humanitarian lead in relation to the 2015 migration crisis showed a different approach. It was not however replicated by any other European states, whose responses were generally highly disappointing, with much talk but very little action. In this respect, Europe failed a profound moral test: what do you do when, as a large bloc of mainly rich countries, you are faced with an almost unprecedented humanitarian crisis, involving poor people of different cultures from disfavoured parts of the world? Europe's overall response was unedifying. Rather than working together to find immediate as well as medium- and longer-term solutions, the unresolved migration and refugee crisis was the catalyst for soul searching: on the European Union ("What is it good for?"), Europe's nation-states ("Who should have the right to be their members?"), and Europeans in general ("What is our view of fellow human suffering in the brunt of very serious and prolonged political and economic disruptions?"). In short, 2015's international migration/refugee crisis openly exposed Europe's previously mostly latent divisions and its organisational ineptitude. Together, these served to fuel centrifugal political pressures across Europe, whose ultimate impact on the EU may not end with Brexit alone while fuelling the spread and political clout of neo-nationalism.

According to Hassan Abedin, head of the Muslim Minorities Division of the Organisation of Islamic Cooperation,

> Right-wing populism in Europe and elsewhere is driven by socio-economic inequality and malaise of political leadership, disenfranchisement, [and] failure of liberal political elites to offer a satisfying

vision of the future. In addition, Europe has historically been relatively homogenous compared to Africa or Asia. The discovery of differences is of the West's making and globalisation has become a conduit of 'dark undertones'.

> (Author's interview #14, with senior official of the Organisation of Islamic Cooperation's Muslim Minorities Division, London, 20 June 2018)

Abedin is highlighting some of the reasons for the political advance of neo-nationalism in both Europe and the USA. In Europe, the international migration crisis of 2015 helped endow previously marginal nationalist and populist parties and politicians with an unprecedented level of authority and legitimacy, in the same way and for the same reasons that Donald Trump was able to attract and retain a high level of electoral support, especially among the 'dispossessed'. As already discussed in this book, such people are often un- or under-employed white men in low-level, unskilled, or semi-skilled jobs, mostly lacking a college education, who have seen their current positions and future prospects diminish as a result of both the effects of globalisation ("exporting jobs from America") and the large numbers of sometimes illegal immigrants from Mexico and Central America who are often prepared to work for less in diminished conditions than indigenous Americans (Jackson, 2016). Many such people appear to believe in Trump's clarion call to "make America great again".

While in America anti-globalisation and anti-immigration zealots rallied around Trump's divisive rhetoric, in Europe a key component of the EU endeavour – the passport-free Schengen area created in 1995 – was in disorder. Following the 2015 immigration crisis, Schengen was suspended in February 2016. How and/or when it would be reinstated was unclear. Across much of Europe, rather than a dismantling of border controls, there was widespread societal reinstatement, in response to both the influx of international migrants and refugees and a seeming Europe-wide incapacity to police the region's borders effectively. What was required and what must be done to improve things in this regard was both a workable desire and practical policies to significantly strengthen and improve the management and security of Europe's borders. This was necessary to assure voters that Europe's leaders not only have the will, but also the capacity to increase the region's security, if 'only' to keep terrorists and illegal migrants out.

The 2015 international migration and refugee crisis made it crystal clear that Europe was not a hermetically sealed rich person's club, able to keep the world's woes away through a policy of benign neglect. A combination of the continuing refugee/migration crisis coupled with unprecedented fears across the region linked to extremism and terrorism brought it home to many

96 Conclusion

European politicians and voters that the region could not any longer shield itself from the political and economic travails of many countries in the Global South. This was especially the case in relation to geographically contiguous regions, including the Middle East, western Asia, and sub-Saharan Africa, all of which contain extensive areas undergoing pronounced state weakness, economic travails, societal fragmentation, and terrorist outrages. Europe responded, on the one hand, with a much-critiqued deal with Turkey to try to curtail the flow of refugees and migrants across the Aegean Sea. In addition, the EU dangled the carrot of increased development aid to sub-Saharan countries to encourage African states to take back migrants not entitled to asylum in Europe. Ultimately, however, such deals, even if successful (which is doubtful), were no more than temporary dressings for a wound: migrants and refugees' determined efforts to reach the promised land of Europe from the Middle East and sub-Saharan Africa would not significantly diminish until the latter regions were safer (in a security sense) and more prosperous, so that most people – rather than an elite few – felt that they were benefiting from economic growth and societal peace.

Despite much talk, including about refugee quotas for each EU member state, Europe did not cover itself in glory. What many regarded as a shabby deal with Turkey seemingly undermined Europe's much-cherished human rights principles. Terrorism and fears of terrorism fuelled neo-nationalist concerns about migrants and immigrants, apprehension that quickly became mainstream and ubiquitous and which politicians almost everywhere in Europe seemed to feel duty-bound to respond to, vying with each other to appear as 'tough' as possible in relation to popular concerns. As already noted, this was also the approach taken by Donald Trump in the USA with highly unexpected electoral success, notably among white Republican voters, both religious and secular. Across both Europe and in the USA, identity politics were clearly in the ascendant, and the result was increased political polarisation between the neo-nationalists, on the one hand, and liberals and progressives, on the other. This is not to deny or overlook the many signs and signals of unity and sympathy for fellow human beings which many in Europe evinced following the 2015 international migration/refugee crisis. In response, across the region, numerous selfless people responded to the crisis with significant and continuing efforts to distribute food and clothes, while some in addition offered shelter in their own homes to migrants and refugees. Several years later, however, issues raised by the summer 2015 international refugee and migrant crisis showed no clear signs of being dealt with or overcome by Europe's elected politicians. In the USA the result of the November 2016 presidential election seemed to indicate what kind of country many Americans now appeared to want their nation to be: not one that was open and welcoming to incomers – that is, of course, the founding philosophy of the USA – but one that sought to create new official barriers to those seeking to emigrate to the country, even for legitimate reasons, especially if they were Muslims or 'Mexicans'.

The concerns in Europe are similar, but at the same time different. On the one hand, the notion of a liberal Europe is enshrined in the European Union and its founding values: a borderless region practising free movement of people seems to many to make good economic sense, while also desirable from a social point a view, enabling people to move freely for business, leisure, and family reasons. The key problem, however, is that the burgeoning number of neo-nationalist politicians and parties, both anti-migrant and against most refugees, is gaining both confidence and political influence in many regional countries. Arguments that might once have been influential – such as that Europe needs many thousands of migrants each year for economic reasons and to keep the wheels of commerce turning – no longer seem to have the capacity to persuade as many people as they once did. Now, the talk is increasingly of how can "we" keep "them" out? How can "we" stop "them" from abusing "our" welfare? How can "we" stop "them" from spreading "their" alien, Islamic beliefs and precepts which undermine "our" cherished, foundational, European values and principles?

Europe did not manage to deal with a crisis caused by factors largely beyond its control. Europe could of course theoretically deal with such issues in a security sense – as shown by agreements with Turkey and sub-Saharan Africa over sending migrants and refugees back. As a last resort, this could include building walls – *à la* Trump or Hungary's Viktor Orbán – designed to keep out the unwanted. The state of Israel has pioneered this approach in its dealings with Palestinians. But if one is concerned that Europe keeps its liberal ideals alive, then such a 'solution' is ultimately futile or worse, as it irrevocably coarsens and diminishes politics by denying the capacity of people outside Europe from enjoying the rights and privileges that Europeans take for granted.

Epilogue

The outcome of the 2020 presidential election in the USA did not resolve the problems noted earlier: what values does America represent and who is legitimately welcome in the USA to live and work? While Biden was the clear winner in terms of both the popular and Electoral College votes, Trump's support rose, amounting to nearly half of the more than 145 million Americans who voted. Biden, at 78 years of age, is a likely one-term president and may not have all the answers to the myriad problems of the USA, which the neo-nationalist Donald Trump was able to exploit successfully for his electoral gain in 2016. America will remain a highly divided country whatever Biden is able to achieve during his presidency. The fissures in the country are so clear and perhaps unresolvable by policy initiatives alone that the question is not how will the USA recover its equilibrium and sense of national purpose but whether it is able to do so. Never before in recent history has political and social polarisation been so apparent. Never before in recent history has the means available to repair the damage seemed so limited. Neither side trusts the other and common ground seems to be absent. Biden has the reputation of someone who is willing and sometimes able to find common ground for agreement between Democrats and Republicans. He may well find this very difficult, however, in the aftermath of Trump's 2020 electoral defeat, which many Republicans believe was due to rigging of the election by Democrats, although no evidence was found to support this claim.

Biden's election will not resolve the problems that Trump has exploited. Immigration will remain a controversial issue, as will what the correct place for America is in a fast-changing world. While Islamist terrorism may have been temporarily tamed with the defeat of the Islamic State in Iraq in 2017, there is no certainty that other foci of contention will not emerge. China poses a huge problem for America's progress in international relations, in terms of both diplomacy and economic growth, while at home there seems little chance that the culture wars will be resolved. Finally, the problems that Trump exploited so successfully have not gone away. Neo-nationalism will continue to be an ideological challenge to American presidents and legislatures. It remains to be seen what methods can be adopted to enable the USA to help resolve its domestic problems and to play its part in collective efforts to deal with pressing issues facing humanity.

Notes

1 The Southern Poverty Law Center reported in February 2017, soon after Trump assumed the presidency, that the numbers of "anti-Muslim hate groups" in the USA had tripled between 2015 and 2017, increasing three-fold: from 34 to 101 (www.splcenter.org/).
2 Breitbart is a right-wing news website.
3 See Matthew Bowman at https://religionnews.com/2018/04/19/donald-trump-is-not-a-christian-but-he-knows-what-the-religious-right-needs-to-hear-says-historian/

References

Abramsky, S. (1996) 'Vote redneck', *The Observer, Life Magazine*, 27 October, pp. 16–19.

Adida, Claire D., David L. Laitin and Marie-Claire Valfort (2016) 'Don't Fear Muslim Immigrants. They Aren't the Real Problem', *Foreign Affairs*. http://marienavalfort.com/wp-content/uploads/2017/05/ForeignAffairs2016_VALFORT.pdf. Last accessed 13 May 2019.

Ahmed, Tufayel (2019) 'Trump Pastor Paula White Tells Followers to Give $229 for "Prophetic Instruction" on How to Defeat Their Enemies', *Newsweek*, 15 November.

Alexander, Laura E. (2019) 'The "Christian Left" is Reviving in America, Appalled by Treatment of Migrants', *Salon*, 20 August. www.salon.com/2019/08/19/the-christian-left-is-reviving-in-america-appalled-by-treatment-of-migrants_partner/. Last accessed 13 November 2020.

Allitt, Patrick (2003) *Religion in America Since 1945: A History*. New York: Columbia University Press.

Altshuler, Glenn C. (2016) 'What Are "Judeo-Christian" Values? Analyzing a Controversial Term', *Washington Jewish Week*, 1 December. http://washingtonjewishweek.com/34907/judeo-christian-values/news/national-news/. Last accessed 13 April 2017.

Americans United (n.d.) 'Project Blitz: A Secret Political Movement Sweeping through the States'. www.au.org/tags/project-blitz. Last accessed 13 November 2020.

Anti-Defamation League (2013) 'Stop Islamization of America (SIOA)'. www.adl.org/sites/default/files/documents/assets/pdf/civil-rights/stop-islamization-of-america-2013-1-11-v1.pdf. Last accessed 3 July 2019.

Bacevich, Andrew (2020) 'Freedom Without Constraints: How the US Squandered its Cold War Victory', *The Guardian*, 7 January. www.theguardian.com/news/2020/jan/07/freedom-without-constraints-how-the-us-squandered-its-cold-war-victory. Last accessed 13 November 2020.

Barker, Jeremy (2020) 'Advancing Religious Freedom for All Requires a Multi-Faceted, Global Effort', *Real Clear Religion*, 19 June. www.realclearreligion.org/articles/2020/06/19/advancing_religious_freedom_for_all_requires_a_multi-faceted_global_effort_496522.html. Last accessed 24 June 2020.

Bates, Stephen (2006) 'Wing and a prayer: Religious right got Bush elected – now they are fighting each other', *The Guardian*, 31 May. https://www.theguardian.com/world/2006/may/31/usa.stephenbates

References

Belew, Kathleen (2018) *Bring the War Home: The White Power Movement and Paramilitary America*. Cambridge, MA: Harvard University Press.

Bellah, Robert (1975) *The Broken Covenant: American Civil Religion in Time of Trial*. Chicago: University of Chicago Press.

Bergmann, Eirikur (2020) *Neo-Nationalism. The Rise of Nativist Populism*. London: Palgrave Macmillan.

Bettiza, Gregorio (2019) *Finding Faith in Foreign Policy: Religion and American Diplomacy in a Postsecular World*. Oxford: Oxford University Press.

Beydoun, Khaled A. (2018) *American Islamophobia. Understanding the Roots and Rise of Fear*. Oakland, CA: University of California Press.

Bob, Clifford (2012) *The Global Right Wing and the Clash of World Politics*, Cambridge: Cambridge University Press

Bob, Clifford (2019a) *Rights as Weapons Instruments of Conflict, Tools of Power*. Princeton, NJ: Princeton University Press.

Bob, Clifford (2019b) '"Why Trump's New Commission on Unalienable Rights is Likely to Upset the Human Rights Community", "The Monkey Cage"', *The Washington Post*, 6 June.

Boorstein, Michelle and Sarah Bailey (2020) 'Episcopal Bishop on President Trump: "Everything He Has Said and Done is to Inflame Violence"', *The Washington Post*, 2 June. www.washingtonpost.com/religion/bishop-budde-trump-church/2020/06/01/20ca70f8-a466-11ea-b619-3f9133bbb482_story.html. Last accessed 13 November 2020.

Borger, Julian (2019) 'Donald Trump Denounces "Globalism" in Nationalist Address to UN', *The Guardian*, 19 September. www.theguardian.com/us-news/2019/sep/24/donald-trump-un-address-denounces-globalism. Last accessed 12 November 2020.

Brammer, John Paul (2018) 'Mike Pompeo Still Opposes Gay Marriage. Now He's about to be Secretary of State', *NBC News*, 12 April. www.nbcnews.com/feature/nbc-out/mike-pompeo-still-opposes-gay-marriage-now-he-s-about-n865556. Last accessed 23 June 2020.

Brubaker, Rogers (2016) 'A New "Christianist" Secularism in Europe', *The Immanent Frame* (website). https://tif.ssrc.org/2016/10/11/a-new-christianist-secularism-in-europe/. Last accessed 1 February 2019.

Brubaker, Rogers (2017) 'Between Nationalism and Civilizationism: The European Populist Moment in Comparative Perspective', *Ethnic and Racial Studies,* 40(8): 1191–1226.

Bryant, N. (2015) 'The Decline of US Power', *BBC News*, 10 July. www.bbc.co.uk/news/world-us-canada-33440287. Last accessed 29 September 2015.

Buchanan, Patrick (1992) 'Patrick Joseph Buchanan, "Culture War Speech: Address To The Republican National Convention", 17 August 1992)', *Voices of Democracy*. https://voicesofdemocracy.umd.edu/buchanan-culture-war-speech-speech-text/. Last accessed 12 November 2020.

Bump, Philip (2019) 'Trump Administration Fans Out to Defend Christianity across the Political Spectrum', *The Washington Post*, 14 October. www.washingtonpost.com/politics/2019/10/14/trump-administration-fans-out-defend-christianity-across-political-spectrum/. Last accessed 23 June 2020.

References

Buzan, Barry and Ole Waever (2009) 'Macrosecuritisation and Security Constellations: Reconsidering Scale in Securitisation Theory', *Review of International Studies*, 35: 253–276.

Calamur, Krishnadev (2017) 'A Short History of "America First"', *The Atlantic*, 21 January. www.theatlantic.com/politics/archive/2017/01/trump-america-first/514037/. Last accessed 13 November 2020.

Campbell, Colin (2016) 'Trump: "Islam Hates Us"', *Business Insider*, 10 March. http://uk.businessinsider.com/donald-trump-islam-hates-us-2016–3?r=US&IR=T. Last accessed 14 February 2019.

'Can American Nationalism Be Saved? A Debate with National Review Editor Rich Lowry' (2019) www.vox.com/policy-and-politics/2019/11/22/20952353/trump-nationalism-america-first-rich-lowry. Last accessed 12 November 2020.

Casey, Shaun (2017) 'How the State Department Has Sidelined Religion's Role in Diplomacy', *Religion & Politics*. https://religionandpolitics.org/2017/09/05/how-the-state-department-has-sidelined-religions-role-in-diplomacy/. Last accessed 23 June 2020.

Casey, Shaun (2020) 'Sojourners', 15 June. https://sojo.net/articles/gap-between-trumps-record-and-rhetoric-religious-freedom. Last accessed 24 June 2020.

Chang, Semoon (2006) 'The North Korean Human Rights Act of 2004', *North Korean Review*, 2(1): 80–88.

Chapman, Roger, and James Ciment (eds.) (2013) *Culture Wars: An Encyclopedia of issues, viewpoints and voices*, New York: M.E. Sharpe.

Christerson, Brad and Christopher Flory (2017) *The Rise of Network Christianity: How Independent Leaders are Changing the Religious Landscape*. Oxford: Oxford University Press.

Clark, Ian (1997) *Globalization and Fragmentation*. Oxford: Oxford University Press.

Clarkson, Frederick (2020) 'The Battle for the Bible Against Christian Nationalism Seeks to Continue Historic Campaign', *Religion Dispatches*, 27 February. https://religiondispatches.org/the-battle-for-the-bible-against-christian-nationalism-seeks-to-continue-historic-campaign/. Last accessed 16 November 2020.

Connor, Walker (1994) *Ethnonationalism: The Quest for Understanding*. Princeton, NJ: Princeton University Press.

Cooper, Melanie (2015) 'The Theology of Emergency: Welfare Reform, US Foreign Aid and the Faith-Based Initiative', *Theory, Culture and Society*, 32(2): 53–77.

Crary, Robert (2019) 'Trump Steadily Fulfills Goals on Religious Right Wish List', *AP News*, 20 August. https://apnews.com/c8626c6bdbab4e3f8232ea1499a6954b. Last accessed 13 November 2020.

Daigle, Delton T., Josephine Neulen and Austin Hofeman (2019) *Populism, Nativism, and Economic Uncertainty. Playing the Blame Game in the 2017 British, French, and German Elections*. Basingstoke: Palgrave Macmillan.

D'Antonio, Michael and Peter Eisner (2018) *The Shadow President: The Truth About Mike Pence*. New York: St. Martin's Press.

Dearden, Lizzie (2017) 'Emmanuel Macron Claims Africa Held Back By "Civilisational" Problems and Women Having "Seven Or Eight Children"', *The Independent*, 11 July. www.independent.co.uk/news/world/europe/emmanuel-macron-africa-development-civilisation-problems-women-seven-eight-children-colonialism-a7835586.html. Last accessed 13 February 2019.

DeHanas, Daniel Nilsson and Marat Shterin (2018) 'Religion and the Rise of Populism', *Religion, State and Society*, 46(3): 177–185.

Desjardins, Jeff (2020) 'All of the World's Wealth in One Visualization', *Visual Capitalist*. www.visualcapitalist.com/all-of-the-worlds-wealth-in-one-visualization/. Last accessed 6 November 2020.

de Tocqueville, Alexis (1969) *Democracy in America*. New York: Doubleday.

Diamond, Sarah (2000) *Not by Politics Alone: The Enduring Influence of the Christian Right*. New York: Guilford Press.

DiMaggio, Anthony R. (2019) *Political Power in America. Class Conflict and the Subversion of Democracy*. Albany, NY: State University of New York Press.

Dobson, James (2019) James Dobson Responds to 'Christianity Today's' Call for Trump Removal. AL.com Alabama. December 23. https://www.al.com/news/2019/12/dr-james-dobson-responds-to-christianity-todays-call-for-trump-removal.html

Doherty, Carroll (2017) 'Key Takeaways on Americans' Growing Partisan Divide Over Political Values', Pew Research Center, 5 October. www.pewresearch.org/fact-tank/2017/10/05/takeaways-on-americans-growing-partisan-divide-over-political-values/. Last accessed 13 November 2020.

Ekström, Mats, Marianna Patrona, and Joanna Thornborrow (2018) 'Right-Wing Populism and The Dynamics of Style: A Discourse-Analytic Perspective on Mediated Political Performances', *Palgrave Communications*, 4(83): 1–11.

'Executive Order on Establishing the President's Advisory 1776 Commission' (2020) www.whitehouse.gov/presidential-actions/executive-order-establishing-presidents-advisory-1776-commission/. Last accessed 13 November 2020.

FP Editors (2019) 'What Trump Promised Duda', June 13. https://foreignpolicy.com/2019/06/13/what-trump-promised-duda/

Farr, Thomas (2001) 'Roots of the International Religious Freedom Report', *Issues of Democracy*. Electronic Journal of the U.S. Department of State, 6(2): 6–10.

Farr, Thomas (2008) *World of Faith and Freedom: Why International Religious Liberty Is Vital to American National Security*. Oxford: Oxford University Press.

Fea, John (2018) *Believe Me. The Evangelical Road to Donald Trump*. Grand Rapids: William Eerdmans Publishing Company.

Federal Register (2019) 'Estimates of the Voting Age Population for 2018', 4 October. www.federalregister.gov/documents/2019/10/04/2019-21663/estimates-of-the-voting-age-population-for-2018. Last accessed 12 November 2020.

Federal Register (2020) 'Advancing Religious Freedom', 2 June. www.federalregister.gov/documents/2020/06/05/2020-12430/advancing-international-religious-freedom. Last accessed 12 November 2020.

Ford, Liz (2019) 'US Accused of Trying to Dilute Global Agreements on Women's Rights', *The Guardian*, 18 March. www.theguardian.com/global-development/2019/mar/18/us-accused-of-trying-to-dilute-international-agreements-un-commission-status-of-women. Last accessed 23 June 2020.

Forster, Dion (2019) 'New Directions in Evangelical Christianities', *Theology*, 122(4): 267–275.

Fox, Jonathan (2016) *The Unfree Exercise of Religion. A World Survey of Discrimination against Religious Minorities*. Cambridge: Cambridge University Press.

References

Fox, Jonathan (2020) *Thou Shalt Have No Other Gods Before Me*. Cambridge: Cambridge University Press.

Freidman, Lisa (2017) 'Syria Joins Paris Climate Accord, Leaving Only U.S. Opposed', *The New York Times*, 7 November. www.nytimes.com/2017/11/07/climate/syria-joins-paris-agreement.html. Last accessed 28 August 2020.

Friedman, Saul S. (1973) *No Haven for the Oppressed. United States Policy Towards Jewish Refugees, 1938–1945*. Detroit: Wayne State University Press.

Gagné, André (2019) 'The Christian Right's Efforts to Transform Society', *The Conversation*, 24 July.

Galli, Mark (2019) 'Trump Should be Removed from Office', *Christianity Today*, 19 December.

García, Mario (2018) 'Nativist, Anti-Immigrant Sentiment in The US has a Long History', *National Catholic Reporter*, 27 June. www.ncronline.org/news/opinion/ncr-today/nativist-anti-immigrant-sentiment-us-has-long-history. Last accessed 14 February 2019.

Gaston, K. Healan (2020) *Imagining Judeo-Christian America. Religion, Secularism, and the Redefinition of Democracy*. Chicago: University of Chicago Press.

Gellner, Ernest (1983) *Nations and Nationalism*. Ithaca: Cornell University Press.

Gerais, Reem (2017) 'Burwell v. Hoppy Lobby (2014)', *The Embryo Project Encyclopedia*. https://embryo.asu.edu/pages/burwell-v-hobby-lobby-2014. Last accessed 28 August 2020.

Gevisser, Mark (2020) *The Pink Line: The World's Queer Frontiers*. London: Profile Books.

Glendon, Mary Ann (2010) 'God and Mrs Roosevelt', *First Things*. May 15. https://www.firstthings.com/article/2010/05/god-and-mrs-roosevelt

Green, John C., Mark J. Rozell and Clyde Wilcox (2003) *The Christian Right in American Politics: Marching to the Millennium*. Georgetown: Georgetown University Press.

Green, John C., Corwin E. Smidt, J. Guth and L. Kellstedt (2005) *The American Religious Landscape and the 2004 Presidential Vote: Increased Polarization*. Washington, DC: The Pew Forum on Religion & Public Life.

Greven, Thomas (2016) *The Rise of Right-Wing Populism in Europe and the United States. A Comparative Perspective*. Washington, DC: Friedrich Ebert Foundation.

Guerrero, Jean (2020) *Hatemonger: Stephen Miller, Donald Trump, and the White Nationalist Agenda*. New York: William Morrow.

Haberman, Clyde (2018) 'Religion and Right-Wing Politics: How Evangelicals Shaped Elections', *The New York Times*, 28 October. www.nytimes.com/2018/10/28/us/religion-politics-evangelicals.html

Hacker, Jacob S. and Paul Pierson (2005) *Off Center. The Republican Revolution & the Erosion of American Democracy*. New Haven: Yale University Press.

Halper, S. and J. Clarke (2004) *America Alone: The Neo-Conservatives and the Global Order*. Cambridge: Cambridge University Press.

Hart, John (2017) 'Is Ideology Becoming America's Official Religion?', *Forbes*, 30 November. www.forbes.com/sites/johnhart/2017/11/30/is-ideology-becoming-americas-official-religion/#2214f043164b. Last accessed 28 August 2020.

Haselby, Sam (2017) 'What Politicians Mean When they Say the United States was Founded as a Christian Nation', *The Washington Post*, 4 July. www.washingtonpost.com/news/posteverything/wp/2017/07/04/what-politicians-mean-when-they-say-america-was-founded-as-a-christian-nation/. Last accessed 28 August 2020.

104 References

Hayes, Luz (2019) 'Personal Email to Author from Liz Hayes, Assistant Director of Communications, Americans United for Separation of Church and State', 15 August 2019, attributed to Alex J. Luchenitser, associate legal director of AU.

Haynes, Jeffrey (1998) *Religion in Global Politics*. Harlow: Longman.

Haynes, Jeffrey (2005a) *Comparative Politics in a Globalizing World*. Cambridge: Polity.

Haynes, Jeffrey (2005b) 'Al-Qaeda: Ideology and Action', *Critical Review of International Social and Political Philosophy*, 8(2): 177–191.

Haynes, Jeffrey (2007) *An Introduction to Religion and International Relations*. Harlow: Pearson Education.

Haynes, Jeffrey (2008) 'Religion and a Human Rights Culture in America', *The Review of Faith & International Affairs*, 6(2): 73–82.

Haynes, Jeffrey (2016) ' "Expert Comment": "National Sovereignty, Globalisation and Securitisation of International Migration", "Expert Commentary" ', Dialogue of Civilizations Research Institute, 29 September. http://doc-research.org/aug19/product/national-sovereignty-globalisation-and-securitisation-of-international-migration/. Last accessed 13 November 2020.

Haynes, Jeffrey (2017) 'Donald Trump, "Judeo-Christian Values," and the "Clash of Civilizations" ', *The Review of Faith & International Affairs*, 15(3): 66–75.

Haynes, Jeffrey (2018) *The United Nations Alliance of Civilisations and the Pursuit of Global Justice: Overcoming Western versus Muslim Conflict and the Creation of a Just World Order*, New York and Lampeter, Edwin Mellen Press.

Haynes, Jeffrey (2019a) *From Huntington to Trump: Thirty Years of the Clash of Civilizations*. New York: Lexington Books.

Haynes, Jeffrey (2019b) 'From Huntington to Trump: Twenty-five Years of the "Clash of Civilizations" ', *The Review of Faith & International Affairs*, 17(1): 11–23.

Haynes, Jeffrey (2020a) 'Trump and the Politics of International Religious Freedom', *Religions,* 11(8): 385. https://doi.org/10.3390/rel11080385. Last accessed 16 November 2020.

Haynes, Jeffrey (2020b) 'Right-wing Populism and Religion in Europe and the USA', *Religions*. Special Issue, 'Religion, Nationalism and Populism across the North/South Divide Religion', guest edited by Jocelyne Cesari. www.mdpi.com/journal/religions/special_issues/populism. Last accessed 16 November 2020.

Haynes, Jeffrey (2021) 'Religion, Nationalism and Transnationalism', in *Oxford Research Encyclopedia of International Relations*. Oxford: Oxford University Press.

Haynes, Jeffrey, Peter Hough, Shahin Malik and Lloyd Pettiford (2017) *World Politics: International Relations and Globalisation in the 21st Century*, 2nd ed. London: Sage.

Hefner, Robert (2010) 'Rethinking Islam and Democracy', in Timothy Samuel Shah, Alfred Stepan, and Monica Duffy Toft (eds.), *Rethinking Religion and World Affairs*. Oxford: Oxford University Pres, pp. 85–104.

Hertzke, Allen (2006) *Freeing God's Children: The Unlikely Alliance for Global Human Rights*. New York: Rowman and Littlefield.

Hervik, Peter (2011) *The Annoying Difference: The Emergence of Danish Neo-nationalism, Neoracism, And Populism in the Post-1989 World*. New York: Berghahn Books.

References

Hobsbawm, Eric (2021) *On Nationalism*. New York: Little, Brown.

Holpuch, Amanda (2019) 'Trump Aide Stephen Miller Told Bannon Immigration Would "Decimate" America', *The Guardian*, 22 November. www.theguardian.com/us-news/2019/nov/22/stephen-miller-bannon-interview-immigration-america. Last accessed 12 November 2020.

Hunter, James Davison (1991) *Culture Wars: The Struggle to Define America*. New York: Basic Books.

Huntington, Samuel (1993) 'The Clash of Civilizations?' *Foreign Affairs*, 72, 3, pp. 22–49.

Huntington, Samuel (1996) *The Clash of Civilizations and the Remaking of World Order*. Normanton, OK: University of Oklahoma Press.

Huntington, Samuel (2004) *Who Are We? The Challenges to America's National Identity*. New York: Simon & Schuster.

Hurd, Elizabeth Shakman (2015) *Beyond Religious Freedom. The New Global Politics of Religion*. Princeton, NJ: Princeton University Press.

Husser, Jason (2020) 'Why Trump is Reliant on White Evangelicals', *Brookings*. www.brookings.edu/blog/fixgov/2020/04/06/why-trump-is-reliant-on-white-evangelicals/. Last accessed 16 November 2020.

ISPU (2018) 'American Muslim Poll 2018: Pride and Prejudice Featuring the First-Ever National American Islamophobia Index'. www.ispu.org/wp-content/uploads/2018/04/American-Muslim-Poll-2018.pdf. Last accessed 14 May 2019.

Jackson, Alex (2016) 'Mexico to USA Migration'. https://geographyas.info/population/mexico-to-usa-migration/. Last accessed 12 November 2020.

Jacoby, William G. (2014) 'Is There a Culture War? Conflicting Value Structures in American Public Opinion', *American Political Science Review*, 108(4): 754–771.

Jethani, Skye (2016) 'Christianity Leads to Atheism'. https://skyejethani.com/trump-and-the-heresy-of-christianism/. Last accessed 13 February 2019.

Jews for a Secular Democracy (2019) 'Why "Judeo-Christian" Values are Problematic'. https://jfasd.org/2019/10/why-judeo-christian-values-are-problematic/. Last accessed 24 June 2020.

Jones, Robert P. and Daniel Cox (2017) *America's Changing Religious Identity. Findings from the 2016 American Values Atlas*. Washington, DC: Public Religions Research Institute.

Jones, Tobias (2018) 'The Fascist Movement That Has Brought Mussolini Back to the Mainstream', *The Guardian*, 22 February. www.theguardian.com/news/2018/feb/22/casapound-italy-mussolini-fascism-mainstream. Last accessed 14 February 2019.

Joustra, Robert (2016) 'Is the Problem Really Religious Freedom?', *The Review of Faith & International Affairs*, 14(3): 129–133.

Juergensmeyer, Mark (ed.) (2005) *Religion in Global Civil Society*. Oxford: Oxford University Press.

Kamali, Mohammad Kashim (2015) *The Middle Path of Moderation in Islam*. New York: Oxford University Press.

Kedourie, Elie (1993) *Nationalism*. Hoboken: John Wiley.

Keohane, Robert (2002) 'The Globalization of Informal Violence, Theories of World Politics, and the "Liberalism of Fear"', *Dialog-IO* (Spring): 29–43.

References

Kitschelt, Herbert (1997) *The Radical Right in Western Europe. A Comparative Analysis*. Ann Arbor: University of Michigan Press.

Koronowski, Ryan (2018) 'This is What Trump's Really Talking about When he Says he's a Nationalist', *Think Progress*, 23 October. https://archive.thinkprogress.org/trump-nationalist-what-does-that-mean-8e477076e155/. Last accessed 12 November 2020.

Kuenkler, Mirjam, John Madeley and Shylashri Shankar (eds.) (2019) *A Secular Age Beyond the West: Religion, Law, and the State in Asia, the Middle East, and North Africa*. Cambridge: Cambridge University Press.

Lamb, Chris (2020) 'President Trump Is No Ronald Reagan', *Inside Sources*, 14 April. www.insidesources.com/president-trump-is-no-ronald-reagan/. Last accessed 12 November 2020.

Lewis, Andrew R. (2017) *The Rights Turn in Conservative Christian Politics: How Abortion Transformed the Culture Wars*. Cambridge University Press.

Lewis, Andrew R. (2019) 'The Transformation of the Christian Right's Moral Politics', *The Forum*, 17(1): 25–44.

Lewis Taylor, M. (2005) *Religion, Politics and the Christian Right: Post-9/11 Powers in American Empire*. Minneapolis: Augsburg Fortress Publishers.

Lind, Michael (2001) 'Nationalism and its Discontents', *Washington Monthly*, 1 December. https://washingtonmonthly.com/2001/12/01/nationalism-and-its-discontents/. Last accessed 12 November 2020.

Lobasz, Jennifer K. (2019) 'Contemporary Approaches to Human Trafficking', in *Constructing Human Trafficking. Human Rights Interventions*. Cham: Palgrave Macmillan.

Lowry, Rich (2019) *The Case for Nationalism. How it Made us Powerful, United and Free*. New York: Broadside Books.

Luhrmann, Anna and Steffan Lindberg (2019) 'A Third Wave of Autocratization is Here: What is New about it?', *Democratization*, 26(7): 1095–1113.

Lynch, Suzanne (2019) 'Trump Condemns "Globalists" in Nationalistic Speech at UN', *The Irish Times*, 24 September. www.irishtimes.com/news/world/us/trump-condemns-globalists-in-nationalistic-speech-at-un-1.4029008. Last accessed 12 November 2020.

Malice, Michael (2018) 'Alt-Right Bible "Camp of The Saints" Proves Everyone's Still Insane', *The Observer*, 2 May. https://observer.com/2018/05/the-insanity-of-alt-right-bannon-aroved-the-camp-of-the-saints/. Last accessed 14 February 2019.

Mann, Windsor (2019) 'How Pat Buchanan Made President Trump Possible', *The Week*, 26 July. https://theweek.com/articles/853163/how-pat-buchanan-made-president-trump-possible. Last accessed 12 November 2020.

Marchetti, Raffaele (2016) *Global Strategic Engagement*. Lanham, MD: Lexington Books.

Marsden, Lee (2020) 'International Religious Freedom Promotion and US Foreign Policy', *Religions,* 11: 260.

McAlister, Melani (2019) 'American Evangelicals, the Changing Global Religious Environment, and Foreign Policy Activism', *The Review of Faith and International Affairs*, 17(2): 1–12.

McQuarrie, Michael (2017), 'The revolt of the Rust Belt: place and politics in the age of anger', *British Journal of Sociology, Special Issue:* The Trump/Brexit Moment: Causes and Consequences, 68, S1, S120–S152.

References

McVeigh, Rory and Kevin Estep (2019) *The Politics of Losing. Trump, the Klan, and the Mainstreaming of Resentment.* New York: Columbia University Press.

Mead, Walter Russell (2010) 'God's Country?', in Timothy Samuel Shah, Alfred Stepan, and Monica Duffy Toft (eds.), *Rethinking Religion and World Affairs.* Oxford: Oxford University Pres, pp. 247–261.

Mead, Walter Russell (2017) 'The Jacksonian Revolt. American Populism and the Liberal Order', March/April https://www.foreignaffairs.com/articles/united-states/2017-01-20/jacksonian-revolt

Mencimer, Stephanie (2020) 'Evangelicals Love Donald Trump for Many Reasons, But One of Them Is Especially Terrifying', *Mother Jones*, 23 January.

Metzner, Michael (2020) 'For God and Country: Essays on Religion and Nationalism', *Genealogy*. Special Issue. www.mdpi.com/journal/genealogy/special_issues/religion.

Miller, Daniel D. (2019) 'The Mystery of Evangelical Trump Support?', *Constellations,* 26: 43–58.

Miller, Eric (2020) 'Trump's Unholy Alliances: An Interview with Sarah Posner', *Religion & Politics*, 29 July. https://religionandpolitics.org/2020/07/29/trumps-unholy-alliances-an-interview-with-sarah-posner/?utm_source=R%26P+Master+List&utm_campaign=da024579c0-Weekly_RSS_Campaign_2017_12_15_COPY_01&utm_medium=email&utm_term=0_05ad9d7d17-da024579c0–104893117. Last accessed 12 November 2020.

Milton, Daniel (2017) 'Does the Cure Address the Problem? Examining the Trump Administration's Executive Order on Immigration from Muslim-majority Countries Using Publicly Available Data on Terrorism', *Perspectives on Terrorism*, 11(4). www.terrorismanalysts.com/pt/index.php/pot/article/view/625. Last accessed 13 May 2019.

Mittelman, Jon (1994) 'The Globalization Challenge: Surviving at the Margins', *Third World Quarterly*, 15(3): 427–441.

Moran, Andrew (2021) 'The US: Security in the Post-9/11 Era', in Peter Hough, Andrew Moran, Bruce Pilbeam and Wendy Stokes (eds.), *International Security Studies. Theory and Practice*, 2nd ed. London: Routledge, pp. 365–374.

Mudde, Cas (2007) *Populist Radical Right Parties in Europe*. Cambridge: Cambridge University Press.

Mudde, Cas (2016) *On Extremism and Democracy in Europe*. London: Routledge.

Muirhead, Russell and Nancy L. Rosenblum (2019) *A Lot of People are Saying. The New Conspiracism and the Assault on Democracy*. Princeton, NJ and Oxford: Princeton University Press.

NDS (National Defense Strategy) (2017) https://www.defense.gov/Explore/Spotlight/National-Defense-Strategy/

National Organizations United in Opposition to Project Blitz and Similar Legislative Efforts (2019) 'Statement From 43 National Organizations United in Opposition to Project Blitz and Similar Legislative Efforts'. www.au.org/sites/default/files/2019-02/Organizations%20Opposed%20To%20Project%20Blitz%202.1.19.pdf. Last accessed 12 November 2020.

Norman, James (2018) 'Christian Soldiers Marching on the US with "Project Blitz"', *The Sydney Herald*, 15 June. www.smh.com.au/world/north-america/christian-soldiers-marching-on-the-us-with-project-blitz-20180608-p4zkbt.html. Last accessed 12 November 2020.

References

NPR (2017) 'Pat Buchanan On "America First" Under Trump', 22 January. www.npr.org/2017/01/22/511048811/pat-buchanan-on-america-first-under-trump?t=1598437262615. Last accessed 12 November 2020.

Nye, Joseph (2002) 'Globalism versus Globalization', *The Globalist* ('The Daily Online Magazine on the Global Economy, Politics and Culture'), 15 April. www.theglobalist.com/StoryId.aspx?StoryId=2392. Last accessed 13 April 2006.

O'Connell, David (2015) *God Wills it. Presidents and the Political Use of Religion*. New Brunswick: Transaction Publishers.

Peaceful Coexistence (2016) 'Peaceful Coexistence Reconciling Nondiscrimination Principles with Civil Liberties. A Briefing before The United States Commission on Civil Rights Held in Washington, DC. Briefing Report'. https://www.usccr.gov/pubs/docs/Peaceful-Coexistence-09-07-16.PDF

Pew Research Center (2014) 'Detailed Tables on the Evangelical Electorate'. https://assets.pewresearch.org/wp-content/uploads/sites/12/2016/03/FT_16.03.14.EvangelicalVote2.pdf. Last accessed 12 November 2020.

Pew Research Center (2016) 'How the Faithful Voted: A Preliminary 2016 Analysis'. www.pewresearch.org/fact-tank/2016/11/09/how-the-faithful-voted-a-preliminary-2016-analysis/. Last accessed 5 October 2018.

Pew Research Center (2017) 'Muslims and Islam: Key Findings in The U.S. And Around the World'. www.pewresearch.org/fact-tank/2017/08/09/muslims-and-islam-key-findings-in-the-u-s-and-around-the-world/. Last accessed 12 February 2019.

Pew Research Center (2018) 'Religion and Public Life'. www.pewforum.org/religious-landscape-study/. Last accessed 5 October 2018.

Pew Research Center (2019) 'In U.S., Decline of Christianity Continues at Rapid Pace', 17 October. www.pewforum.org/2019/10/17/in-u-s-decline-of-christianity-continues-at-rapid-pace/. Last accessed 12 November 2020.

Philpott, Daniel (2020) 'Ignore the Optics. Trump's Executive Order Could Jumpstart the Cause of Global Religious Freedom', *America. The Jesuit Review*. www.americamagazine.org/politics-society/2020/06/09/trump-executive-order-global-religious-freedom. Last accessed 24 June 2020.

Piacenza, Joanna (2019) 'White Evangelicals' Support for Trump Has a Soft Underbelly', *Morning Consult*, 1 May. https://morningconsult.com/2019/05/01/white-evangelicals-support-for-trump-has-a-soft-underbelly/. Last accessed 24 June 2020.

PRRI (2020) 'Summer Unrest over Racial Injustice Moves the Country, but Not Republicans or White Evangelicals', 21 August. www.prri.org/research/racial-justice-2020-george-floyd/. Last accessed 13 November 2020.

Reiffer, B. (2003) 'Religion and Nationalism: Understanding the Consequences of a Complex Relationship', *Ethnicities*, 3(2): 215–242.

Robbins, T. and D. Anthony (eds.) (1982) *In God We Trust New Patterns of Religious Pluralism in America*. New Brunswick: Transaction Publishers.

'Ronald Reagan's Commitment to Make America Great Again' (2020) www.reagan.com/ronald-reagans-commitment-to-make-america-great-again?__cf_chl_jschl_tk__=c2b7297eec317c036be52551a1bbd908a24a8aca-1605109189-0-AYviZZD_YT6R1G_1CFoud5avS66KHNKYUD3eNS6t3IHJ6gqzScfAJHQH5aygXaHCTAet4lrqouoZfR2u5dmuJW4HjWnCja3xobTKjvedacEAp4-oTp

Cq45x_lBCJN28UMXZNB5Y-OetCGLIC_8i_P7ySNt1lWpC308F32cbtAj0u20
210of2z8IBrsNgVnyET-Vb6ecRetOjp1fYh8Nnr20HD3X8eX-NZ0tZ85z7_iqu
8HZfZ3Kb5jHCk2Bykm3r7dCrvVfyuZ_uEnmLWldY7Y0L_PJnHq069Z8P7Y-
0wz2nT1TzLUEOKExgobyNwSHEXN84hcy5QNeZy1vYYd3z85o. Last accessed 16 November 2020.

Rosenberg, Paul (2018) 'Onward, Christian Soldiers: Right-wing Religious Nationalists Launch Dramatic New Power Play', *Salon*, 29 April.

Runnymede Trust, The (1997) *Islamophobia: A Challenge for Us all*. London: The Runnymede Trust.

Ryan, Ben (2018) 'Christianism: A Crude Political Ideology and the Triumph of Empty Symbolism', *Religion and Global Society*. https://blogs.lse.ac.uk/religionglobalsociety/2018/11/christianism-a-crude-political-ideology-and-the-triumph-of-empty-symbolism/. Last accessed 13 February 2019.

Sarna, Jonathan D. (1982) 'Jews, the Moral Majority, and American Tradition', *Journal of Reform Judaism* (Spring): 1–8.

Schwartz, Matthias (2019) 'The "Religious Freedom" Agenda. Trump-administration Officials are Using a Two-word Phrase as a Rhetorical Swiss Army Knife on the World Stage', *The Atlantic*, 16 July. www.theatlantic.com/politics/archive/2019/07/trump-administration-religious-freedom/594040/. Last accessed 24 June 2020.

Shai, Hanan (2020) 'The 2020 US Presidential Election: A Seminal Moment in Western History', Bar-Il University, BESA Center Perspectives Paper No. 1,716. https://besacenter.org/perspectives-papers/us-presidential-election-2020/. Last accessed 24 June 2020.

Sherratt, Timothy (2019) 'The Religious Problem with Religious Freedom', *The Review of Faith & International Affairs*, 17(1): 119–121.

Shimron, Yonat (2018) 'A Campaign to Blitz the Country in "In God We Trust" Laws Takes Root', *National Catholic Reporter*, 3 July. www.ncronline.org/news/politics/campaign-blitz-country-god-we-trust-laws-takes-root. Last accessed 24 June 2020.

Siddiqui, Sabrina (2019) 'Steve King, White Supremacy and The Problem With Donald Trump', *The Guardian*, 20 January. www.theguardian.com/us-news/2019/jan/20/steve-king-is-representative-of-the-problem-with-donald-trump. Last accessed 13 February 2019.

Sides, John, Michael Tesler and Lynn Vavreck (2019) *Identity Crisis. The 2016 Presidential Campaign and the Battle for the Meaning of America*. Princeton, NJ: Princeton University Press.

Smith, Anthony D. (1972) *Theories of Nationalism*. New York: Harper & Row.

Smith, Anthony D. (2003) *Chosen Peoples. Sacred Sources of National Identity*. Oxford: Oxford University Press.

Smith, Bradley (2017) 'The Imaginary Reagan Revolution: On the Conservative Undermining of Radical Left-Wing Discourse', *Transatlantica*, (1). https://journals.openedition.org/transatlantica/8847. Last accessed 12 November 2020.

Smith, David (2020) 'Pardons sink Trump further into swamp of his own shamelessness' https://www.theguardian.com/us-news/2020/dec/23/pardons-sink-trump-further-into-swamp-of-his-own-shamelessness

Smith, Samuel (2019) 'National Association of Evangelicals Elects Walter Kim as its First Minority President', *The Christian Post*, 17 October.

Smith, Terry (2020) *Whitelash. Unmasking White Grievance at the Ballot Box*. Cambridge: Cambridge University Press.

Soper, J. Christopher and Joel Fetzer (2018) *Religion and Nationalism in Global Perspective*. Cambridge: Cambridge University Press.

Srinivasan, Sharath (2014) 'Negotiating Violence: Sudan's Peacemakers and the War in Darfur', *African Affairs*, 113(450): 24–44.

Stewart, Katherine (2020) *The Power Worshippers. Inside the Dangerous Rise of Religious Nationalism*. London: Bloomsbury.

Sullivan, Andrew (2013) 'The Decline and Fall of Christianism', *The Dish*, 23 October. http://dish.andrewsullivan.com/2013/10/23/the-decline-and-fall-of-christianism/. Last accessed 13 February 2019.

Svitych, Alexander (2018) 'Populism or Neo-nationalism? Political Observer on Populism'. https://populismobserver.com/2018/04/30/populism-or-neo-nationalism/. Last accessed 16 November 2020.

'The 1619 Project' (2020) www.nytimes.com/interactive/2019/08/14/magazine/1619-america-slavery.html. Last accessed 16 November 2020.

Theodore, John (2019) *Survival of the European (Dis)Union. Responses to Populism, Nativism and Globalization*. Basingstoke: Palgrave Macmillan.

Tóibín, Colm (2020) 'Review of Mark Gevisser's *The Pink Line*', *The Guardian*, 20 June. www.theguardian.com/books/2020/jun/20/the-pink-line-by-mark-gevisser-review-the-worlds-queer-frontiers. Last accessed 23 June 2020.

Tondo, Lorenzo (2018) 'Italy's Matteo Salvini Joins Bannon's European Populist Group', *The Guardian*, 8 September. www.theguardian.com/world/2018/sep/08/italy-matteo-salvini-joins-steve-bannon-european-popullist-group-movement. Last accessed 5 October 2018.

'Transcript of Reagan's Farewell Speech to American People' (1989) *The New York Times*, 12 January. www.nytimes.com/1989/01/12/news/transcript-of-reagan-s-farewell-address-to-american-people.html. Last accessed 13 November 2020.

Van Engen, Abram (2020) 'White Evangelicals and the New American Exceptionalism of Donald Trump', *Religion & Politics*, 29 September. https://religionandpolitics.org/2020/09/29/white-evangelicals-and-the-new-american-exceptionalism-of-donald-trump/. Last accessed 13 November 2020.

Verma, Pranshu (2020) 'Pompeo's Human Rights Panel Could Hurt L.G.B.T. and Women's Rights, Critics Say', *The New York Times*, 23 June.

von Beyme, Klaus (1988) 'Right-wing Extremism in Post-war Europe', *West European Politics*, 11(2): 1–18.

Wald, Kenneth (1991) 'Social Change and Political Response the Silent Religious Cleavage in North America', in George Moyser (ed.), *Religion and Politics in the Modern World*. London: Routledge, pp. 239–284.

Walt, Stephen (2011) 'The Myth of American Exceptionalism', *Foreign Policy* https://foreignpolicy.com/2011/10/11/the-myth-of-american-exceptionalism/

Warburg, M. (2001) 'Religious Organisations in a Global World. A Comparative Perspective', University of Copenhagen, Denmark. Paper presented at the 2001 International Conference, 'The Spiritual Supermarket: Religious Pluralism in the 21st Century', 19–22 April, London School of Economics, Houghton Street, London WC2A 2AE.

Wessner, David (2003) 'Addressing Fundamentalism by Legal and Spiritual Means', *Human Rights and Human Welfare*, 3: 65–76.

Whitehead, Andrew and Samuel Perry (2020) *Taking America Back for God: Christian Nationalism in the United States*. Oxford: Oxford University Press.

Whitehead, Andrew, Samuel Perry and Joseph O. Baker (2018) 'Make America Christian Again: Christian Nationalism and Voting for Donald Trump in the 2016 Presidential Election', *Sociology of Religion*, 79(2): 147–171.

Wiebe, Robert (2002) *Who We are*. Princeton, NJ: Princeton University Press.

Wise, Alan (2020) 'Trump Announces "Patriotic Education" Commission, a Largely Political Move', *NPR*, 17 September. www.npr.org/2020/09/17/914127266/trump-announces-patriotic-education-commission-a-largely-political-move?t=1603813333149. Last accessed 13 November 2020.

Wolfe, Dawn R. (2019) 'One Nations Under Their God: Project Blitz is Still in Business, Including in Michigan', *Daily Kos*, 5 December. www.dailykos.com/stories/2019/12/5/1903709/-One-nation-under-their-God-Project-Blitz-is-still-in-business-including-in-Michigan. Last accessed 23 June 2020.

Wong, Edward (2019) 'The Rapture and the Real World: Mike Pompeo Blends Beliefs and Policy', *The New York Times*, March 30, 2019

Woodhouse, Leighton Akio (2018) 'Trump's "Shithole Countries" Remark is at the Center of a Lawsuit to Reinstate Protections for Immigrants', *The Intercept*, 29 June. https://theintercept.com/2018/06/28/trump-tps-shithole-countries-lawsuit/. Last accessed 16 November 2020.

Ziv, Ronen, Amanda Graham and Liqun Cao (2019) 'America First? Trump, Crime, and Justice Internationally', *Victims & Offenders*, 14(8): 997–1009.

Zubovich, Gene (2018) 'The Christian Nationalism of Donald Trump', *Religion & Politics*, 17 July. https://religionandpolitics.org/2018/07/17/the-christian-nationalism-of-donald-trump/. Last accessed 16 November 2020.

Author's personal interviews

1 Senior official, International Organisation for Migration, New York, 19 June 2017.
2 Former US Department of State's acting special envoy to the Organisation of Islamic Cooperation Washington, DC, 17 April 2018.
3 State Department diplomat with 23 years' experience in the Middle East and North Africa, Washington, DC, 17 April 2018.
4 Co-founder and executive director of Muslim Public Affairs Committee, Washington, DC, 17 April 2018.
5 Former White House press secretary and currently Washington-based communications consultant, Washington, DC, 19 April 2018.
6 Senior official of the Brooking Institution and former US State Department member, Washington, DC, 24 April 2018.
7 Former US diplomat and Distinguished Professor in the Practice of Diplomacy School of Foreign Service, Georgetown University, Washington, DC, 24 April 2018.

8 Personal interview with consultant to the Holy See, Georgetown University, Washington, DC, 24 April 2018.
9 Former US special representative for religion and global affairs and director of the US Department of State's Office of Religion and Global Affairs, Washington, DC, 24 April 2018.
10 Senior member of Brooking Institution and former US Department of State, Washington, DC, 24 April 2018.
11 Senior Pakistan diplomat, Washington, DC, 25 April 2018.
12 Senior official of Center for Muslim-Christian Understanding, Georgetown University, Washington, DC, 25 April 2018.
13 Academic and expert on international migration, Maria Grzegorzewska University, Warsaw, Poland, in Berlin, 19 June 2018.
14 Senior official of the Organisation of Islamic Cooperation's Muslim Minorities Division, London, 20 June 2018.

Index

1619 Project 57
1776 Commission 57, 58

abortion 7, 16, 38, 39, 41, 43, 51, 52, 54, 62, 68
Afghanistan 23, 79
African-Americans 4, 12, 47, 48
Al-Qaeda 22, 24, 34, 36, 71
'America First' (slogan) 1, 8, 49, 52, 59, 72, 74
America First nationalism/nationalists 2, 7, 8, 10–14, 15, 36, 50, 52, 59, 61, 67, 70, 84
American Legislative Exchange Council 63, 68
Americans United for Separation of Church and State (AU) 63, 66, 67

Bachmann, Michelle 66
Bannon, Stephen 55, 88–89
Barr, William 65, 75
Bellah, Robert 46–47
Bergmann, Eirikur 27, 29
Berlin Wall, fall of 22, 94
Biden, Joe 17, 41, 87, 97, 98
Black Lives Matter 57, 84
Brazil 25, 28, 89, 92
Brubaker, Rogers 26, 27, 91, 92
Buchanan, Pat 48, 49, 54
Burwell v. Hobby Lobby 63
Bush, George H. W. 34, 39, 45, 49
Bush, George W. 1, 16, 30, 34, 72, 78, 79, 83

Canada 2, 54
Central America 11, 13, 33, 55, 88, 95
China 2, 14, 17, 33, 54, 58, 67, 74, 75, 82, 84, 85, 88, 98
Christian conservatives 6, 14, 36
Christianism/Christian civilisationism 92, 93
Christian nationalism/nationalists 8–10, 15, 16, 17, 29, 30, 50, 52, 67, 68, 70, 80, 84, 88, 89, 90
Christian Right, the 2, 15, 19, 36, 37, 40, 43, 47, 49, 52, 60
Christocentric approach to international religious freedom 83
Civil religion (USA) 39, 46, 52, 61
Clarkson, Frederick 64, 65
clash of civilisations thesis 14, 15, 18, 26, 56, 57
Clinton, Bill 16, 34, 49, 61, 77, 78, 79, 83
Clinton, Hillary 1, 40, 49
Cold War, the 34, 48, 60, 71, 72, 75
Commission on Unalienable Rights 83
Congressional Prayer Caucus Foundation 64, 68
coronavirus (Covid-19) pandemic 7, 14
culture 27, 30
culture wars in the USA 6, 13, 16, 19, 36, 42, 45–51, 62, 70

democracy 17, 20, 22, 26, 27, 32, 34, 70, 71, 75, 77, 81
Democratic Party 5, 10, 14, 41, 71, 74, 98
Diamond, Sara 39
Dobson, James 86
dominionist theology 64, 65
Duda, Andrzej 83

Index

education 3, 8, 39, 52, 57–59, 62, 82
employment and jobs in America 4, 5, 11, 53, 54, 67, 93, 95
equality 25, 45
Europe 15, 28, 29, 41, 89, 94, 96
European Union, the 2, 15, 17, 20, 32, 54, 73, 94, 96, 97
Evangelical Advisory Board 66, 67

Faith & Opportunity Initiative 66, 67
Farr, Thomas 61, 80, 86
First Amendment of US constitution 42, 61, 63
France 32, 91
Frank R. Wolf International Religious Freedom Act (2016) 79

Germany 32, 94
global economic crisis (2008) 4, 27
globalisation 12, 13, 14, 22, 26, 30–32, 40, 48, 55, 95
globalism/globalists/anti-globalists 5, 11, 12, 13, 14, 22, 31, 32–33, 40, 75, 93
Green v. Connolly 44

Hart-Cellar Act of 1965 13–14, 44
Hobsbawm, Eric 21, 2
human rights 16, 20, 26, 27, 32, 34, 38, 39, 41, 71, 72, 77, 82, 86
Hungary 25, 91
Hunter, Davison James 36, 37
Huntington, Samuel 14, 15, 26, 90, 91

immigration, legal/illegal 3, 4, 13, 14, 16, 25, 28, 29, 30, 36, 50, 53, 55, 56, 59, 73, 88, 93, 95, 96, 98
immigration reform 55–57
India 6, 8, 23, 25, 28, 92
internationalism 20, 21
international religious freedom 16, 29, 76, 86
International Religious Freedom Act (IRFA) 76–80, 86
International Religious Freedom Alliance 83, 85
Iran 17, 74, 75, 76
Iran hostage crisis of 1979 6
Islamic extremism/terrorism 3, 10, 27, 71, 75, 88, 96, 98

Islamic State (ISIS) 22, 24, 75, 79, 98
Islamophobia 9, 18
Israel 8, 9, 75, 97

Jackson, Andrew 13, 73
Jews 25, 28, 43, 78, 86, 91
Judeo-Christian values 40, 43, 47, 55, 57, 58, 59, 64, 68, 82, 83, 84, 90, 93

Kennan, George 73, 74
King, Steve 55, 90
Know-Nothings (US political party) 3, 49

LGBTQ+ issues 15, 16, 19, 38, 39, 45, 47, 51, 52, 62, 63, 79, 82, 83, 84
liberal international order (LIO) 70, 71
liberals 7, 12, 15, 19, 36, 45, 49, 93

Macron, Emmanuel 32, 90, 91
'make America great again' (slogan) 1, 2, 5, 6, 11, 17, 52, 53–55, 59, 61, 89, 95
Merkel, Angela 32, 94
Mexico/Mexicans 2, 3, 4, 5, 7, 11, 13, 14, 16, 17, 50, 53, 54, 55, 59, 73, 88, 90, 91, 95, 97
Mexico City policy ('global gag rule') 83
Miller, Stephen 50, 55, 88
Ministerial on Advancing Religious Freedom 83, 85
modernisation theory 41
Modi, Narendra 22, 92
Moral Majority/Jerry Falwell 43, 44, 45, 47
Muslim-Americans 10, 25, 60, 62
Muslims/Islam 1, 9, 10, 11, 14, 28, 29, 33, 36, 50, 53, 55, 56, 57, 59, 88, 89, 90, 91, 93, 97

National Association of Evangelicals 18, 38
National Defense Strategy (NDS) 74–75
nationalism 5, 8, 19, 21
National Security Strategy (NSS) 74–75, 80
nativism/nativists 3, 5, 9, 27, 28, 29, 34, 35, 57

Index

Nazi Germany 21, 72, 76, 77
Near East and South Central Asia Religious Freedom Act (2014) 79
neo-nationalism: and America's international relations 70–86; and culture wars 36–51; development of 19–35; in the USA 52–69
new world disorder 22
new world order 21
North Korea Human Rights Act (2004) 78

Obama, Barack 1, 16, 30, 34, 45, 54, 60, 72, 75, 78, 79, 83
Orbán, Viktor 22, 25, 91, 92, 97

Pakistan 23, 79, 82, 85
partisanship 7, 15, 19, 40, 46, 50, 61, 68, 78, 79, 80
Pence, Mike 34, 41, 62, 65, 75
Poland 15, 25, 83
Pompeo, Mike 33, 34, 41, 62, 65, 71, 75, 77, 83, 84, 85
populism 5, 10, 27, 28, 34, 48, 49
prayers (Christian) 7, 43, 47, 50, 62
presidential election 2016 13, 52, 96
presidential election 2020 97
President's Emergency Plan for AIDS Relief (PEPFAR) 79
Project Blitz/Freedom for All 16, 62–67, 68
Protestant Evangelicals 2, 10, 37, 39, 44, 78

Raspail, Jean (*The Great Replacement*) 89
Reagan, Ronald 1, 6, 7, 16, 17, 18, 19, 29, 44, 45, 49, 53, 58, 67, 76
religion, public role of 42
religious freedom (USA) 3, 16, 17, 34, 50, 62, 63, 67, 70, 71
religious nationalism 5, 23, 24
Republican Party 1, 5, 6, 7, 10, 15, 19, 39, 40, 44, 45, 48, 71, 98
Roe v. Wade 44
Roosevelt, Eleanor 86
Russia 6, 8, 23, 25, 74, 75, 84
Rust Belt states 4, 5, 14

Saudi Arabia 23, 75, 85, 86
secular (white) conservatives 2, 3, 41

secularisation 9, 37, 39, 42, 43
secularists 12, 45, 53, 67
secular state 24, 43
September 11 2001 ('9/11') 4, 22, 23, 24, 27, 34, 36, 62, 71, 75, 93
Seven Mountains Mandate 65
sexual and gender equality 3
sharia law 10, 59
Smith, Anthony D. 21, 23
Soviet Union 12, 18, 19, 20, 22, 27, 48, 72
Stewart, Katherine 60
Sudan Peace Act (2002) 78
Supreme Court, the 40, 41, 44, 47, 50, 62, 63, 88
Syria, civil war in (2015-) 27, 84, 94, 96

Tea Party, the 53, 54, 55
Trafficking Victims Protection Act (2000) 78
Trump, Donald: 1776 Commission 57, 58; 'America First' (slogan) 1, 8, 49, 52, 59, 72, 74; America First nationalism/nationalists 2, 7, 8, 10–14, 15, 36, 50, 52, 59, 61, 67, 70, 84; Christian nationalism/nationalists 8–10, 15, 16, 17, 29, 30, 50, 52, 67, 68, 70, 80, 84, 88, 89, 90; Evangelical Advisory Board 66, 67; Faith & Opportunity Initiative 66, 67; globalism/globalists/anti-globalists 5, 11, 12, 13, 14, 22, 31, 32–33, 40, 75, 93; immigration, legal/illegal 3, 4, 13, 14, 16, 25, 28, 29, 30, 36, 50, 53, 55, 56, 59, 73, 88, 93, 95, 96, 98; immigration reform 55–57; Islamic extremism/terrorism 3, 10, 27, 71, 75, 88, 96, 98; Judeo-Christian values 40, 43, 47, 55, 57, 58, 59, 64, 68, 82, 83, 84, 90, 93; 'Make America Great Again' (slogan) 1, 2, 5, 6, 11, 17, 52, 53–55, 59, 61, 89, 95; Muslims/Islam 1, 9, 10, 11, 14, 28, 29, 33, 36, 50, 53, 55, 56, 57, 59, 88, 89, 90, 91, 93, 97; National Association of Evangelicals 18, 38; presidential election 2016 13, 52, 96; presidential election 2020 97; Republican Party 1, 5, 6, 7, 10, 15, 19, 39, 40, 44, 45, 48, 71, 98
Turkey 2, 6, 8, 74, 82, 83, 84, 96

Uighurs (China) 16, 82, 85
United Nations, the 13, 15, 16, 17, 32, 33, 38, 61, 70, 71, 72, 75, 76, 77, 83, 86
United States Constitution (1788) 77
United States Constitution, First Amendment of 8, 42, 61, 63
Universal Declaration of Human Rights (1948) 16, 70, 77, 83, 86

Vietnam War, the 9, 18, 47

Wald, Kenneth 41, 42, 45, 46, 47
Wallnau, Lance 65
White-Cain, Paula 66
white Catholic conservatives 2, 7, 40
white Christian conservatives 2, 51, 60
white Christian nationalists 7, 40
white power/supremacy 4, 93
women's rights 7, 15, 54, 63, 68, 79, 83

Yugoslavia 22, 23